D1058036

a little light

a little light

20 ways the coronavirus response could make the world better

Tom Whipple, Sarah Knapton,
Lucy Mangan, Alex Hern, Lindsay Dodgson
introduction by Graham Davey

sphere

SPHERE

First published in Great Britain in 2020 by Sphere

3 5 7 9 10 8 6 4 2

Typeset in Garamond by M Rules
Printed and bound in Great Britain by Clays Ltd, Elcograf S.p.A.

Papers used by Sphere are from well-managed forests
and other responsible sources.

Sphere
An imprint of
Little, Brown Book Group
Carmelite House
50 Victoria Embankment
London EC4Y 0DZ

An Hachette UK Company
www.hachette.co.uk

www.littlebrown.co.uk

CONTENTS

INTRODUCTION

PROFESSOR GRAHAM DAVEY

In December 2019, stallholders in a seafood market in Wuhan in central China began to fall ill with an as-yet-unknown virus. The market not only sold seafood but also traded illegally in wild animals, including marmots, pangolins, birds, rabbits, bats, snakes and a number of other animals renowned in China for their medicinal properties. Soon the mystery illness began to spread rapidly, and on 1 January 2020 the Wuhan market was shut down for inspection and cleaning. But it was too late. Coronaviruses are known to be highly transmittable between humans and animals and this new version, found in humans and named Covid-19, had a genetic make-up more than 90 per cent identical to that of a coronavirus found in bats and pangolins. These animals are the motley suspects for the origin of the world coronavirus outbreak – an outbreak that was confirmed as a global pandemic by the World Health Organization on 11 March 2020.

The pandemic has had a significant impact on the lives of almost every human being on the planet. It has created economic havoc, taken away the livelihoods of significant numbers of workers worldwide and has summarily and devastatingly shortened the lives of thousands of people across the globe. The absurdity of the reach and impact of this pandemic was emphasised, with some poetic licence, on Twitter with the tweet 'Mind blowing how some boy in China ate a bat, and it eventually led to the postponement of Elgin v Brechin'![1]

As soon as the seriousness of the epidemic was understood and it became apparent how quickly coronavirus was being transmitted between human beings, many countries began to instigate lockdowns in an attempt to stem its spread. On 10 March Italy became the first European country to impose a nationwide lockdown on its 60 million inhabitants, quickly followed by lockdowns in Spain, France, Belgium and the United Kingdom. By the beginning of April almost a third of the global population was on coronavirus lockdown, including large parts of the world's most populous countries, such as India and the United States.

A deadly virus on the loose is one thing, but a lockdown brings with it unprecedented threats and challenges to the average person. Added to the fear of infection and maybe even death was a whole swathe of stressful and anxiety-triggering events imposed almost overnight and without warning. Most lockdowns were introduced within only hours of being announced, so few people had time to adjust to the new reality before their daily routines and life-priorities were turned upside down.

Anxiety is an adaptive emotion that has proved its worth over thousands of years of evolution by gearing people up to deal more effectively with potential threats and challenges in their lives.[2] And the coronavirus lockdown brought with it many immediate threats and challenges. The comforting things we had taken for granted for most of our lives were now taken away from us – our routines, certainty, unlimited access to provisions, the opportunity to earn an income, even the opportunity to meet up with friends, family and loved ones – and the future was suddenly somewhere at the end of a very dark, unfathomable tunnel.

So, as lockdowns were introduced, we would have expected to see anxiety and stress as an immediate response to this challenging new reality. And that is what we saw – albeit in a very measured way. Professor Richard Bentall and his colleagues at the University of Sheffield carried out a survey of 2000 people between Monday 23 March (the day of the UK government's lockdown announcement) and Friday 27 March.[3] Prior to the announcement, 16 per cent of those in the survey reported significant anxiety, but on the day immediately after the announcement this had risen to 36 per cent – more than 1 in 3 people were suddenly reporting clinically significant levels of anxiety and stress. The spike in stress and anxiety to the lockdown was quite possibly a result of shock following the sudden and somewhat unexpected announcement, but then, for the remainder of that week, anxiety levels immediately fell, with just over 20 per cent reporting significant anxiety on each subsequent day. In normal times, national surveys reliably indicate that 1 in 5 of the UK adult population experiences clinically significant anxiety;[4] Professor Bentall's survey shows that this level was raised to 1 in 3 on the introduction of a lockdown but within a day or so it returned to normal levels, with the majority of people appearing to be resilient and faring relatively well.

There are people who are particularly vulnerable to stress and anxiety during unusual times such as a pandemic lockdown. The Sheffield University survey was able to identify a number of different sufferers in this group: people aged under thirty-five, people living in a city, those living alone or with children, with lower incomes, with health conditions, and those whose incomes had already been hit by the pandemic prior to the lockdown. This is only reasonable and to be expected. And in addition to those whose anxieties were triggered by the specific effects of the pandemic and the lockdown, there are those with particular psychological characteristics that make them even more likely to be badly affected.

Even prior to the pandemic, there were also many people living lonely lives – and loneliness is a significant source of stress and anxiety that is only likely to be exacerbated during a lockdown. Why does loneliness matter so much in a pandemic lockdown? It matters because human beings have evolved to be social animals, so a lack of social contact will itself be a source of stress and chronically lonely people tend to have higher blood pressure and are more vulnerable to infections.

Apart from the physical risks of loneliness, many of its significant effects are psychological ones. John Cacioppo at the University of Chicago has spent many years researching how loneliness can compromise psychological and physical well-being. His findings show that loneliness increases risk of suicide, increases perceptions of stress and results in less restorative sleep. In terms of physical effects, loneliness raises levels of the anxiety hormone cortisol and, over long periods, can increase the risk of mortality to a level comparable with smoking fifteen cigarettes a day.[5]

So what about the threat of the Covid-19 virus itself? If the challenges of a lockdown don't affect your anxiety levels, then the fear of contracting a new and potentially deadly virus may do. There are two groups of people who are particularly vulnerable to this: those with a pre-existing health anxiety, a fear of becoming ill, and, more specifically, those with an obsessive-compulsive contamination fear, in which the sufferer has developed complex rituals and routines designed to eliminate any opportunities for contamination by germs or viruses (a condition often characterised by obsessive-compulsive washing). Paradoxically, for those who have a health anxiety or OCD contamination fears, a pandemic lockdown can be a good thing in disguise. It gives a sufferer much more control over their fears by limiting who will bring potential germs and viruses into their homes, and the monotony of a lengthy lockdown allows those who've developed complex cleaning and washing rituals to get on with those rituals without interruption from outside activities. What's more, in the case of a global pandemic, their worst fears have already happened, so it's now possible to stop being in a state of anxious apprehension.

Staying with the theme of a good thing in disguise, it seems that many people who suffer anxiety and depression reported an improvement in their symptoms after the pandemic lockdown began. Grace Weinstein had been diagnosed with panic disorder, an anxiety condition in which the sufferer experiences frequent unpredictable and debilitating panic attacks. But after the lockdown things seem to change: 'when I wake up, I don't feel sluggish as I normally do. I find it easier to get out of bed,' she said. 'The intrusive thoughts that normally buzz around my brain like flies on a feeding frenzy have disappeared. My family is healthy, I tell myself. I am healthy . . . Despite everything, I realize, I am OK. More OK than I have been in years.'[6]

For many people this unexpected bonus in unprecedented times can be explained. In Grace's case, she suffers panic attacks, and in many cases this type of attack occurs in situations where the person feels stressed and needs to find a 'safe' place in order to avoid these stressors. That safe place will often be the person's own home (you can see where this is going). A lockdown will prevent many people with a panic-type anxiety condition leaving their 'safe' place – a relief and reassurance for them.

There are many reasons why a lockdown may provide some

respite to those with pre-existing conditions of anxiety and depression, rather than exacerbating their fears. For example, if you fear the world as a dangerous and challenging place, being ordered to stay away from it for an indefinite time is a godsend. It provides relief from all those day-to-day stressors that generate chronic anxiety. For many, a global pandemic also puts those daily anxieties into perspective and provides time to reflect on what really matters in life – that petty argument with your boss is now a trivial memory compared to losing an income or losing a life. Then there's the comfort of gathering social support, as everyone rallies round in a time of need. Social support is a powerful palliative for most mental health problems, and even if this is provided indirectly via phone conversations, social media, WhatsApp groups, email or videoconferencing, it will be a source of comfort for those with fragile mental health.

But things make us anxious only to the extent to which we view them as threats and challenges and, in the context of a global pandemic, what was previously a threat may no longer feel like one, and what was previously a challenge may become a life-saver. Take technofear. During normal times, the technophobe would find many ingenious ways to escape the demands of new technology, but during a lockdown, technology becomes an essential means of staying connected – whether by smartphone or videoconferencing, for social purposes or to enable working from home. The pandemic lockdown is forcing technophobes to 'face their fear' – a process that is a tried-and-tested stalwart of all anxiety remedies. It works because having to engage with what they fear forces the anxious individual to discover that what they fear is not as threatening or as challenging as they had imagined.

In addition, during a lockdown crisis there is a mixture of emotions, many of which may challenge anxiety for a place in your life. Supportive friends and family, and a safe home, can foster gratitude and hope – positive emotions that can replace anxiety and its associated threats and challenges. People can sit down and put their anxieties into perspective, which they previously wouldn't have had time to do, due to the constant distractions of everyday life.

Human beings are a species that won't just grit their teeth and get through a cataclysmic pandemic lockdown with a good old dose of wartime spirit; we're just as likely to build on our innovations and insights during a crisis as we are simply to go back to our old ways once a danger has passed.

Such crises change values, provide new perspectives and turn what were troublesome hassles into irreplaceable necessities. For example, who were the people we revered and valued prior to the pandemic? Celebrities, entrepreneurs, entertainers, writers and footballers may have come near the top of the list, but not so much now. The new high-profile heroes are intensive-care nurses, supermarket shelf-stackers, bus drivers and altruistic neighbours. We are suddenly aware of how the world needs those who tirelessly support the basic structures of everyday life.

And what a new perspective we have on technology.

Perpetual connectivity was often seen as a curse – creating, rather than calming, anxieties. Our obsession with the internet and all it has spawned gave us FOMO (fear of missing out), fake news and feelings of disconnectedness and failure when we saw the so-called perfect lives of vloggers and our 'friends' on social media. Our obsession with 'connecting' woke us up in the morning and made sure it was the last thing we did at night before we fell asleep.

Then along came a global pandemic and overnight the internet turned from being a niggling obsession that interfered with our real lives – to *being* our real lives. Suddenly we need the internet so we can work remotely; social media now helps to dispel fake news instead of simply creating it; doctors and nurses diagnose illnesses and calm patients via a video link instead of a rushed ten-minute consultation in a busy GP's surgery. Perhaps most startling is the fact that people halfway around the world are as close to us as our next-door neighbours – we can share a video-drink with a friend in Los Angeles or Singapore as easily as with a friend who lives just a few streets away.

It remains to be seen how these practical consequences of the coronavirus pandemic survive beyond the crisis. But the situation has changed our views of what are anxieties and threats, it has provided entirely new perspectives on old activities, and it has forced us to reappraise our views of who and what is valuable in society. There are many questions that only the future will answer. Will physical mass gatherings become a rarity? Will the handshake become a greeting of the past? Will family video calls replace the weekend visit by Grandma and Grandpa? And will we all appreciate endangered species purely for their contribution to nature rather than for the so-called medicinal value of their meat?

Notes

1. https://twitter.com/pieandbov/status/1238435249744424960
2. Davey, G., *The Anxiety Epidemic*, Robinson, 2018, Chapter 1
3. https://www.sheffield.ac.uk/news/nr/depression-anxiety-spiked-aft...-announcement-coronavirus-mental-health-psychology-study-1.885549

    'Depression and Anxiety Spiked After Lockdown Announcement, Coronavirus Mental Health Study Shows', University of Sheffield, 31 March 2020
4. Davey, G., *The Anxiety Epidemic*, Robinson, 2018, Chapter 3
5. Davey, G., *The Anxiety Epidemic*, Robinson, 2018, Chapter 3
6. https://www.thedailybeast.com/coronavirus-is-making-a-lot-of-people-anxious-and-depressed-but-some-sufferers-actually-feel-better-now

    Bradley, L., 'The Coronavirus Pandemic is a Devastating Mass Trauma – But Some People With Anxiety and Depression Have Seen Their Symptoms Improve', *The Daily Beast*, 27 April 2020

SOCIAL MEDIA'S TIME TO SHINE

ALEX HERN

Something unusual happened in the San Francisco Bay Area in February.

The Bay was always quite a target for the burgeoning pandemic. The technology industry's close links with China, both as a manufacturing hub and supplier of some of the sector's most talented engineers, mean that it was receiving travellers from Wuhan right up until the airports were closed. And, of course, it's a dense urban area anyway: in San Francisco proper, people live, work and play in as close proximity as they do in any city around the world, while in Silicon Valley the campus atmosphere, open-plan offices and communal canteens of the large tech companies aren't conducive to social distancing.

It still came as a bit of a surprise to learn quite how exposed the area was. In late April, Santa Clara County, the home of Silicon Valley, reported that a fifty-seven-year-old auditor who had died on 6 February had been infected with coronavirus.[1] Since she hadn't recently left the country, her death suggested that the virus was being transmitted locally far earlier than had previously been thought.

But then the funny thing happened. Despite having all the prerequisites for hosting America's first major Covid-19 cluster, San Francisco ... didn't. The disease remained under control, even though the authorities didn't learn that there was an outbreak for a further twenty days.

How did the region pull off such suppression? At this stage, we can't completely dismiss the potential that it didn't, and that a huge, undiagnosed outbreak is waiting to rear its head in northern California. Nor, if the region did succeed, can we discount simple luck.

But there's a more interesting possibility: perhaps the credit for the limited outbreak should go to Twitter.

It's hard to remember the Before Times, but early February was not a period when reports of the new virus slowly escaping containment in inland China were front-page news across most of the world. If the virus was thought about at all, it was about the effects that a slowdown in China would have on Western economies. 'Social distancing' wasn't a phrase on anyone's lips, and less than a week after California's first death, I found myself the target of gentle mockery when I offered a fist bump rather than a handshake at an interview. Perhaps I should have put my hand on my heart instead.

But if you wanted to care, the information was there. News of life under lockdown in Hubei emerged through posts on China's version of Twitter, Sina Weibo, and through forwarded messages on WeChat. Research papers were written, shared and translated for non-technical audiences, posted to Medium and linked on Twitter. Discussions about how to deal with a slowdown in China swelled to cover the obvious but all-too-unasked question: what if it comes here?

On 13 February, the day after I offered my fist for a dap, it became a trend piece. With the title '"No handshakes, please": The tech industry is terrified of the coronavirus',[2] tech site *Recode* wrote about the growing number of Silicon Valley companies that were taking their own measures against the virus. *Recode* reported that the venture capitalist firm Andreessen Horowitz had posted the headline sign on its front doors; Facebook had cancelled a global marketing summit it had planned in March; and the Stanford Graduate School of Business, 'arguably the world's most elite training ground for budding tech executives and venture capitalists', had cancelled an exchange program with Beijing's Tsinghua University.

These unilateral actions were, in the first instance, in contrast to those taken by the region's authorities – San Francisco's Lunar New Year celebrations went ahead on 8 February, despite opposition – and, later, influential. By 16 March San Francisco had become the first major US city to issue a 'stay at home' order, with the whole of California following a few days later.

Social media also helped fight a communications battle that public health services weren't even aware needed to be fought. On 29 February, *The Economist* published a briefing about the growing crisis in Italy, detailing the country's social distancing measures.[3] It included a chart, adapted from a 2017 paper by the Centers for Disease Control and Prevention titled 'Community Mitigation Guidelines to Prevent Pandemic Influenza',[4] featuring the now-familiar twin-humped visualisation of the spread of an epidemic with, and without, social distancing.

The chart quickly broke loose from its moorings and began spreading on social media. In one image, it showed clearly and cleanly the importance of fighting a pandemic by washing your hands, not touching your face and staying at home: this would help 'flatten the curve'. In March, a third line was added to recreations of the chart, showing 'healthcare system capacity', to explain the value of spreading out the same number of infections over a longer period of time. By the end of the month, it had grown into a cornerstone of the communications strategy around coronavirus. Interactive sites showed the effect of lockdowns on the curve,[5] CNN anchors stood in front of video screens showing the chart,[6] and a novelty T-shirt adapting the slogan to fit a golfing pun raised almost $100,000 for charity.[7]

But the curve still had its roots in traditional media. By contrast, the datapoint that technology analyst Ben Thompson argued was 'the single most influential piece of information'[8] in the early days of coronavirus was a Twitter thread from Trevor Bedford, a member of the Seattle Flu Study team. The researchers had been taking regular samples from infected people in Washington State and, in February, decided to begin analysing them for SARS-CoV-2, the virus that causes Covid-19. What they found was concerning: a series of minor mutations in a recent case matched those on the very first reported case in the USA, which had arrived on 19 January. 'This strongly suggests that there has been cryptic transmission in Washington State for the past 6 weeks,' Bedford wrote on 1 March.[9] 'I believe we're facing an already substantial outbreak in Washington State that was not detected until now due to narrow case definition requiring direct travel to China.'

'You can draw a direct line from this tweet thread to widespread social distancing, particularly on the West Coast,' Thompson wrote a week later. 'Many companies are working from home, traveling has plummeted, conferences are being canceled.'

But the thing about Bedford's thread is that it shouldn't have existed. The Seattle Flu Study was censured by the CDC for overstepping its remit; the thread wasn't peer-reviewed, nor even published as a conventional academic paper to a preprint repository. It was, in short, everything we know to be careful of when it comes to the publication of information online. Except it was true, and it was a warning sign for the US.

Sadly, the success of social media couldn't last. As the crisis grew and attention turned, falteringly and then overwhelmingly, towards any iota of information about Covid-19, the experts were slowly swamped. First came a downgrading in the quality of the 'armchair epidemiologists', as people with increasingly distant expertise weighed in, peaking with Richard Epstein, a legal academic who published an article on 16 March arguing that just 500 Americans would die from coronavirus. Just as Bedford's thread had encouraged office shutdowns across Silicon Valley, so Epstein's blogpost caught the ear of influential figures including, reportedly, Donald Trump himself.[10]

Then came the bona fide misinformation: folk remedies about how to tackle the virus, conspiracy theories about the real reasons for lockdown, repurposed falsehoods about the supposed danger of 5G mobile masts. The internet improves the ability of everyone to speak to everyone else, and that can be used for good or for ill.

But those early victories should not be forgotten. For once, the truth spread around the world while the liars were still getting their boots on.

Notes

1.   https://www.nytimes.com/2020/04/22/us/santa-clara-county-coronavirus-death.html

    Fuller. T., Baker, M., Hubler, S., Fink, S., 'A Coronavirus Death in Early February Was "Probably the Tip of an Iceberg"', *New York Times*, 22 April, 2020

2.   https://www.vox.com/recode/2020/2/13/21128209/coronavirus-fears-contagion-how-infection-spreads

    Ghaffary, S., '"No Handshakes, Please": The Tech Industry is Terrified of the Coronavirus', *Recode*, 13 February 2020

3.   https://www.economist.com/briefing/2020/02/29/covid-19-is-now-in-50-countries-and-things-will-get-worse

    'Covid-19 is Now in 50 Countries, and Things Will Get Worse', *The Economist*, 29 February 2020

4.   https://www.cdc.gov/mmwr/volumes/66/rr/rr6601a1.htm

5.   https://www.nytimes.com/interactive/2020/03/25/opinion/coronavirus-trump-reopen-america.html

    Kristof, N. and Thompson, S. A., 'Trump Wants to "Reopen America." Here's What Happens if We Do.' *The New York Times*, 25 March 2020

6.   https://www.youtube.com/watch?v=EKQ0AasW8yI

    'Are US Efforts to Flatten the Curve Working? CNN's John King Examines', CNN, 29 March 2020

7. https://www.golfdigest.com/story/how-one-apparel-company-raised-over-dollar90000-for-coronavirus-relief-with-a-clever-golf-t-shirt

   Romano, B., 'How One Apparel Company Raised More Than $90,000 for Coronavirus Relief With a Clever Golf T-Shirt', *Golf Digest*, 9 April 2020

8. https://stratechery.com/2020/zero-trust-information/

   Thompson, B., 'Zero Trust Information', *Stratechery*, 11 March 2020

9. https://twitter.com/trvrb/status/1233970559257468928

10. https://www.newyorker.com/news/q-and-a/the-contrarian-coronavirus-theory-that-informed-the-trump-administration

    Chotiner, I., 'The Contrarian Coronavirus Theory That Informed the Trump Administration', *New Yorker*, 30 March 2020

THE BRITISH PSYCHE

LUCY MANGAN

I have a theory that pandemic conditions have been strangely liberating to the British psyche. No touching, for example, is now de rigueur. There are no more anxious negotiations when meeting a friend or acquaintance (does this one shake hands, kiss on the cheek, or on both cheeks? Do I know them as well as I think I do? As well as they think I do? Do they feel they know me better than I think they do? Is it too late to abandon this whole meeting/friendship/job/life that has led me to this vexed point?). These mental entanglements have now been clear-cut by coronavirus. Two metres apart is, I suspect, the distance we were meant to have between us this whole time.

Paradoxically, the pandemic has made it easier to forge real connections – often the first connections – with those who might otherwise have remained strangers. In London (and I believe most large cities, though I can only talk with any kind of authority about the capital, in which I was born and in many of whose various parts I have lived as a roving adult in search of marginally affordable accommodation) this primarily means neighbours. You might live next door to them (cheek by jowl, a mere layer of bricks and mortar separating you!) but, if your work schedules are different, never previously have seen them. You might only fleetingly acknowledge them if you do. You might know their first names but not their surnames. They might speak to you only to let you know they're going on holiday, or you might only ever know they were away when they return with tans and sombreros. It's not universal, this urban isolation, but it is by no means unusual.

But now that isolation is enforced, now that the world's been turned upside down, now that we all have at least one thing – flesh and blood's susceptibility to malevolent microbial forces – in common, what do we find (anecdotally at least)? Communication creeps in! The feeling steals over us: it would be a little absurd, would it not, to remain unsmiling, eyes cast down, away from the person who is suddenly a comrade in adversity?

Perhaps, one begins to think, as the strange times work their strange ways upon one's psyche, it would be ... okay ... permissible ... perhaps even a moral duty ... to ask how they were? And maybe ask the old lady who lives a few doors down, too? Even as an unspoken undercurrent, 'I'm just venturing a gesture and expressing an interest and concern for you because there is at the moment a non-negligible chance you are truly suffering and without intervention will die' is a terrific icebreaker. I am proud of us as a nation that we needed this level of stimulus to breach each other's privacy and that we can do it when required. As forced experiments go, there have been worse.

A friend of mine who has just had a baby has been inundated with cakes, hand-me-down clothes, toys and books from people she has never met but, she reasons, must have seen her out walking with the pram. Diffident notes are often attached, apologising for the intrusion and blaming the 'special circumstances', which suggests these kindnesses might have been felt but not acted upon in pre-Covid days. Another friend has been shocked to learn that the man who lives next to her is on benefits because he has mental health issues that make him unable to leave the house freely and thus render him unemployable. He always presents a perfectly happy, ordinary face to her and she had no idea until he had to ask her to go to the food bank for him. She was even more shocked to learn that he habitually goes hungry if his money runs out or he is not able to get to the shops.

There will, I am sure, be a million other similar stories out there. And if this is happening all over, if these little bridges are being built – connections made where none was before, links forged in a chain that would otherwise never have come into being – is that not a hopeful thing? We live, generally, in an age of division, under a government that seeks it, with a media that shifts its newspapers and generates clicks on its websites by turning demographic against demographic and always finding an 'other' to blame for what, more often than not, are political, systemic problems unsusceptible to individual causation or solution, and which is plugged into social media that are literally designed to cause and thrive on argument and disunity.

To fight back against all that, you need as much ammunition as you can get. And reality is our best weapon. Every face-to-face interaction is a blow struck against the message of hostility that comes at us from all sides. Each shared piece of gossip, each nugget of knowledge passed on (which shop has flour, which supermarket has eggs today), each egg traded for the flour someone else managed to get, or each babygro handed on to someone you've seen passing in the street, gives the lie to the narrative of scarce resources, of life and society as a zero-sum game upon which those with power depend to preserve their positions. Stories of benefit-scroungers and shirkers milking the system become less credible when you know you're living next door to someone who the system does not allow to feed himself more than five days out of seven.

An erosion of prejudice and the presence of empirical, experiential evidence against the 'facts' with which we are customarily presented, and against the attitudes that suffuse our daily lives, makes lies unsustainable. An acceptance of what was previously understood as the norm, we must hope, is now impossible. Time for a new normal.

REBALANCING NATURE

SARAH KNAPTON

On 3 April 2020 residents in the city of Jalandhar in Punjab, India, woke to an astonishing sight. There on the horizon, drenched in the rosy glow of morning sunshine, was the Himalayan mountain range of Dhauladhar, in Himachal Pradesh.

The sacred, snow-laden peaks, which are more than 120 miles away from Jalandhar, had not been seen from there for nearly thirty years, because they had been obscured by a hazy wall of smog. But with citizens banished to their homes, cars stripped from the roads and planes grounded, the 19,650-foot giants – which are said to contain the lake abode of the Hindu god Shiva – could once again assert their place in the landscape.

Near-global lockdown brought unprecedented falls in pollution across the world, from the toxic hotspots of Beijing and Sao Paulo to Italy's undulating Po Valley and the tree-lined suburbs of London. In Delhi, where pollution levels range from eye-watering to life-threatening, residents began to notice unfamiliar bright-blue skies and air of Alpine freshness, and evening stars, long hidden by a blanket of fumes, twinkled into view at nightfall.

As early as February, satellite data was starting to confirm what residents in China were noticing on the ground, with instruments recording dramatic falls in pollution in the country. The city of Wuhan, in Hubei province, where the pandemic began, saw one of the first and largest drops in Co2 and No2 emissions. The seething metropolis of 11 million people serves as a major transportation hub and is home to hundreds of factories supplying car parts and other hardware to global supply chains. But just a few weeks after the January lockdown, fine particulate matter – one of the most dangerous air pollutants – had fallen by 30 per cent, according to readings from the Copernicus Atmosphere Monitoring Service satellite[1]. By the middle of March, nitrogen dioxide – produced from car engines, power plants and other industrial processes – had dropped by 40 per cent, which, according to Paul Monks, Professor of Atmospheric Chemistry and Earth Observation Science at the University of Leicester, was the equivalent of taking 64,000 cars off the road for the three months of lockdown.

China is one of the world's worst polluters, normally belching out up to 40 megatonnes of nitrogen oxides per year – half of Asia's total emissions[2]. So the huge falls were felt beyond its borders, particularly in South Korea, which has battled with pollution blowing in from Chinese factories.

As restrictions were imposed throughout Europe, Madrid, Milan and Rome recorded decreases in nitrogen oxides of around 45 per cent, while Paris saw a dramatic drop of 54 per cent coinciding with the French capital's strict quarantine measures. The changes over northern Italy were particularly striking because smoke from a dense cluster of factories tends to get trapped against the Alps at the end of the Po Valley, making it one of Western Europe's pollution hotspots. But by March huge falls had occurred[3].

Two weeks after the nationwide lockdown was announced on 23 March, in Britain nitrogen dioxide levels had fallen by as much as 60 per cent, and by the beginning of April UK road travel had fallen to levels last recorded in 1955, when Winston Churchill was still prime minister.

And humans were not alone in benefiting from the near-global shutdown.

Just a few weeks into lockdown, the normally murky canals of Venice had transformed into calm, clear-blue waterways, where shoals of tiny silver fish swam and crabs scuttled over the sandy beds replete with plant-life thriving in the streaming sunshine that could finally reach the bottom. Even jellyfish were seen swimming through the translucent waters. Here, it wasn't pollution that was the problem but the waves from water taxis, tourist boats and gondolas churning up the mud on the canal floor, concealing the busy marine world beneath and blocking out the light. Although social media stories of dolphins and swans in the lagoon turned out to be false, there were true reports of cormorants returning to dive for fish now that they could see beneath the water, and ducks making nests on the vaporetto water-bus stops.

Elsewhere, rare leatherback turtles built more nests on Thailand's shores than at any time in the past twenty years, as tourists deserted the beaches. By late March, the Phang Nga national park reported eighty-four hatchlings. Pink flamingo numbers at Albania's Narta Lagoon on the Adriatic coast also increased, up a third during lockdown, as visitors kept away. Curly pelicans also flourished in the area, thanks to the new-found tranquillity.

UK bumblebee populations are expected to thrive this year due to the fall in air pollution, which often disguises the scent of flowers, making it harder for them to find nectar. And with fewer tourists tramping our coastal and rural pathways, the charity Buglife believes beetles could enjoy a record breeding season. The substantial fall in traffic and countryside visitors also brought a welcome respite for ground-nesting birds, with a surge expected for the number of beach-nesting terns, waders and songbirds such as the chiffchaff and skylark, which are often disturbed by dogs and walkers in the breeding season. In Wales, peacocks were seen wandering through Bangor, while goats took the opportunity to congregate on Llandudno's deserted streets and sheep were spotted munching the grass on roundabouts in Monmouthshire.

Fewer cars inevitably lead to less roadkill, saving some of the 100,000 hedgehogs, 30,000 deer, 50,000 badgers and

100,000 foxes that are killed on Britain's highways each year. Amphibians, in particular, can travel more safely to mate and have a better chance of spawning. Figures from Belgium showed that by mid April the usual 2000 reported roadkill deaths of polecats, hedgehogs and badgers was down to just 77.

Hampered by a lack of staff, councils also postponed cutting the grass on roadside verges, allowing wildflowers to thrive and providing a haven for pollinators.

Britain also saw its sunniest-ever April, with reductions in air pollution believed to be partly responsible because particles in the air can seed clouds and obscure sunlight.

The world also became quieter. This lockdown phenomenon was first spotted by Thomas Lecocq, a seismologist at the Royal Observatory of Belgium, in Brussels, who noticed a drop in the constant hum of vibrations in the planet's crust caused by transport networks and human activities. Such a noise reduction usually occurs only at Christmas. Soon, seismologists across the world were noticing the drop, giving them a rare window to take measurements of the planet without much human activity. The Max Planck Institute for Ornithology in Germany has found that chronic traffic noise can damage birds in the egg, so the co-occurrence of lockdown and the mating season could increase the amount of chicks surviving, thereby boosting bird numbers. Noise from ships is known to increase the stress-hormone levels of marine creatures such as whales, so the pause in cruise vessels and bulk carriers could bring them some relief.

Likewise, reduced human activity has been expected to bring falls in industrial water pollution, allowing for ecological recovery, while reduced fishing and the collapse in the seafood export market looks likely to improve numbers of cuttlefish, scampi and scallops. The reduction in the import of goods and produce saw less ballast water discharged into UK waters, limiting the number of invasive species arriving.

A reduction in high-intensity light pollution from warehouses, factories, car parks and outdoor sporting facilities could boost the population levels of nocturnal wildlife.

Undoubtedly this calmer world won't last when our globe slowly reopens for business, but we can still expect to see the first fall in global emissions since the 2008 financial crisis. Maybe this will give people a taste of the air we might breathe in a low-carbon future. And perhaps, post-lockdown, we will be less inclined to put up with dirty cities bereft of the magic of the night sky, the sound of songbirds or the hideaways of our ancestral gods on the horizon.

Notes

1. https://atmosphere.copernicus.eu/amid-coronavirus-outbreak-copernicus-monitors-reduction-particulate-matter-pm25-over-china

    Lopez, N., 'Amid Coronavirus Outbreak: Copernicus Monitors Reduction of Particulate Matter (Pm2.5) Over China', Copernicus, 4 March 2020

2. https://airqualitynews.com/2020/04/17/coronavirus-lockdowns-effect-on-air-pollution-provides-rare-glimpse-of-low-carbon-future/

    Monks, Prof P. 'Coronavirus: Lockdown's Effect on Air Pollution Provides Rare Glimpse of Low-Carbon Future' Air Quality News, 17 April 2020

3. https://airqualitynews.com/2020/03/16/air-pollution-has-fallen-in-northern-italy-following-lockdown/

    Neill, P., 'Air Pollution Has Fallen in Northern Italy Following Lockdown', Air Quality News, 16 March 2020

REMOTE WORKING

ALEX HERN

Impossible things happen daily now, sometimes as many as six before breakfast. They happen because they have to: because if delivery drivers continued not to receive sick pay, they would go to work ill; because if tenants were evicted now, they would be be unable to Stay at Home and Protect the NHS; because if governments tried to balance their budgets, the global economy would collapse and not recover for a generation.

Still, it can be bittersweet to see something you had been assured was impossible suddenly become, well, not.

Working from home has long been a contentious request for many employers. It carries with it the presumption of a level of trust: is this employee one who will actually work from home, or will they bunk off if they're not kept beneath the beady eye of a watchful manager? And it undercuts one of the founding myths of the modern office, that this gathering together of people is more than just a loose collection of minds working with a common goal and is in fact a gestalt entity capable of greatness. If people can stay at home and be just as productive, why have an office at all?

And then, suddenly, the concerns didn't matter. If you could work from home, you did. If you couldn't, maybe you weren't working at all – so all the greater motivation to ensure that as many people as possible fall into the former category. Thankfully, many people do.

2020 is not 1920, nor even 2002. Remote working is different now. The past few decades have seen the rise of technologies, approaches and simple mindsets that make it a very different prospect from the heady days of 'telecommuting'.

Some of these are simply down to better technology. Take videoconferencing: the technology we use today – so widespread and cheap to implement that we can have virtual happy hours, network together whole classrooms for remote story time, or host interactive all-hands meetings with hundreds or thousands of attendees – is a technical marvel.

It relies on the widespread availability of broadband speeds and 4G mobile signal to provide the bandwidth required to pump out that lovely grid of faces you stare at on your fourth essential meeting of the day. Our post-iPhone world means that the webcam, once a specific accessory bought only by those in committed long-distance relationships (or very loose short-term ones) has become ubiquitous at just the right time. And the growth in cheap, flexible processing power is what enabled a company like Zoom to go from 10 million users to 200 million in a single month without simply falling over from the strain.

Similarly, the rise of 'software as a service' was never intended to help remote workers, but it has. Twenty years ago, most business-critical functions were run from a specific server kept in the corner of the office, typically maintained by a specialist contractor with a certification from Microsoft that would keep all the various components up to date. Remote working entailed an expensive and inefficient virtual private network (VPN) set-up, designed to let your computer pretend it was also physically in the office. That approach would never have scaled to the entire workforce, and, even today, companies have had to send warnings out to their employees advising them to only log in to the VPN only if they absolutely must.

Thankfully, we now have alternatives. In 2020, your work, like your life, is probably carried out mostly online. Tools like Salesforce, Gmail and Microsoft Office can all be accessed through a browser; even specialist services that do require a standalone app, from Photoshop to Bloomberg Terminals, are usually provided in ways which allow employees to use them on any device they can get their hands on.

Other improvements are better described as that buzzword of business-school manuals, 'disruptive innovation': the idea that something can be worse than what it's replacing, but if it's also cheaper, more ubiquitous and more accessible, that doesn't matter. How else to describe, for instance, the colleague of mine whose response to being told to stay at home was to buy a £20 Bluetooth keyboard and prop up his phone in landscape position? It's hard to argue that such an experience is better than having a full-blown desktop computer – though he seems perfectly happy – but you can't beat the price. Such flexibility has been crucial to shifting a significant chunk of the economy remotely.

And then there's the parts of working from home that no manager would choose to replicate, but are just as crucial. Take Slack, or its competitors from Microsoft and Google. The software is sold as 'workplace collaboration', yes, and much of what goes on there is precisely that: colleagues asking queries of one another, sending urgent requests for assistance or flagging up problems.

But much ... isn't. There's a reason, for instance, why the default installation of Slack includes a #random channel: it's because so much of what makes an office that gestalt hive-mind has nothing to do with professional tasks, and everything to do with the ability to swing by your friend's desk on the way to the coffee machine, ask them what they're working on, talk about how the weekend went and offer to bring them back a hot drink. You can't do the latter over the internet (yet?) but the secret success of every remote office is in finding ways to smuggle that sort of interaction under the noses of bosses who still secretly dream of perfecting the early-twentieth-century 'scientific management' of Frederick Taylor. My own remote-working set-up includes rooms for board games, video games (very important to keep separate), gardening, cooking, and 'internet stuff'. None are work; all keep me sane.

We are, in short, getting better and better at recreating many of the useful aspects of the office from home, both the obvious and the under-appreciated. That means that what's lost is increasingly the aspects of the office that are . . . less useful.

Most obvious is the death of the commute. Study after study has shown that the easiest route to happiness is spending less time travelling to work: in 2019, research from the University of the West of England showed that 'longer commute times are associated with lower job and leisure time satisfaction, increased strain and poorer mental health'.[1] Adding twenty minutes to a commute had the same negative impacts as slashing salaries by 19 per cent.[2] Overnight, people have seen their commute reduced from hours to the time it takes to shuffle from the breakfast table to their desk – or to just put aside the cereal bowl and open the laptop.

Of course, this isn't the best time for half the world to experience working from home for the first time. Dropping the commute is undoubtedly a positive, but it probably doesn't outweigh the psychological struggle of losing most human contact for months on end. Seasoned home-workers emphasise the importance of getting out of the house periodically, whether that means temporarily decamping to a café or being more rigorous about arranging a full social calendar, but those coping mechanisms are out of the question now.

The same goes for the other great benefit of home working:

childcare. Children are hard to fit around an office job. School starts after the commute needs to begin and finishes well before the end of a working day. Children's needs are unpredictable: they get sick, fall over, and get in trouble. And childcare is expensive. Cripplingly so.

In normal times, home-working can help with these things, but these are not normal times. With the schools closed, a Staying-at-Home parent isn't working uninterrupted from 9:30 to 3:30 and then having to juggle kids for the last few hours of the day; they are teacher, classroom assistant, technical support and canteen staff all rolled into one. It is chaotic.

But the upsides aren't only about what happens today, they're also about what happens next year, and the year after.

Many parents – perhaps even most – might find that they're happy to return to the old way of doing things, having experienced the difficulty of doing it all without help. But some, perhaps for the first time in their careers, will be realising that there is a better way than leaving home before their child is awake and returning after they go to bed.

On 12 May 2020, Jack Dorsey, the CEO of Twitter, emailed employees to tell them that they didn't need to come back to the office. Ever. All employees except those whose work physically required commuting, such as maintaining servers, would be allowed to continue to work from home after the crisis abates. The company is the first of many who will make the change. That sort of flexibility is not quite as impossible as it once seemed.

Notes

1. https://uwe-repository.worktribe.com/output/850689/
   how-commuting-affects-subjective-wellbeing

   Clark, B., Chatterjee, K., Martin, A. and Davis, A, 'How
   Commuting Affects Subjective Wellbeing', *Transportation*, 2019

2. https://www.inc.com/business-insider/study-reveals-commute-
   time-impacts-job-satisfaction.html

   Loudenback, T., 'Study: Adding 20 Minutes to Your Commute
   Makes You As Miserable As Getting a 19 Percent Pay Cut', *Inc.*,
   23 October, 2017

UNIVERSAL HEALTHCARE

TOM WHIPPLE

The clapping started on the streets. It spread along pavements chalk-marked with messages of thanks to doctors and nurses. It passed through blocks of flats, their windows adorned with crepe-paper rainbows and praise for 'our' National Health Service.

At 8 p.m. every Thursday, as hospitals in every community approached capacity, the clapping came. Through the spring of the pandemic, in Downing Street, on Park Lane and in the council blocks in between, people emerged to see neighbours, to see their community together once more, and to clap.

Not since the 2012 Olympics, when the dancers of the opening ceremony spelled out the initials 'NHS' in lights, has there been such a tribute. This time the recognition was a hymn to our true national church in its hour of need.

Whether it made your heart soar or made you feel just the tiniest bit uncomfortable probably depends on your temperament. What is clear is that after this pandemic the place of the NHS in all our affections is assured.

Not, if we are honest, that its place was ever very much threatened. Polls even before the crisis showed there is more support for the NHS than there is for the Queen. The emotional case for a national health service has rarely faltered.

But wash away that chalk and wait for the crepe-paper rainbows to make their way into the recycling bin and something more subtle, but ultimately more powerful, will remain. As well as the emotional case, the pandemic has also made the intellectual case for a universal health service. It has reminded us that this creation, this health behemoth – once famously the world's biggest user of fax machines – is not just about justice or fairness or caring for your fellow man. It has reminded us that the health of a nation – and ultimately each one of us – is always best ensured through the collective: through a system free at the point of delivery and that does not discriminate. As Aneurin Bevan said on the creation of the NHS[1], 'The collective principle asserts that ... no society can legitimately call itself civilised if a sick person is denied medical aid because of lack of means.'

We are not used to thinking of ourselves as a collective, much less as a herd. But in this crisis we have been forced to do so – forced to realise that our individual selves are part of a wider organism. When, early in the outbreak, the government started briefing journalists about 'herd immunity', it was a bad communications strategy but it contained a truth. The only way we leave this is together, as a herd – a herd in which, through immunisation or infection, we have the antibody armour to repel the disease.

Our exit strategy applies to us as a collective but our comeuppance affects us as individuals. Until February, South Korea had stamped out coronavirus completely, isolating the first 30 patients and stopping the spread in a mass national effort. Then Patient 31 was identified and, rather than have her symptoms properly investigated, she decided to go to church. The resulting infections became Patients 32–5048. A single individual had blown the collective strategy apart. This is why testing is so important.

This is also why it was such a catastrophe when, as happened so frequently at the start of the outbreak, patients in the USA decided not to get tested because they could not afford the fees. The test was not a service for them – it would do them little good to know whether they did or did not have a disease, given that there wasn't a cure. The test was for the benefit of everyone else they would meet. That is why it is not only right, but sensible, that the community should pay for the test. You can have the best health insurance in the world, but it will not protect you from a contagious disease. What protects you from a contagious disease is if your whole population – rich and poor – can receive the healthcare they need.

What also protects you is if that healthcare can, just occasionally, come with the heft of the state. You need an organisation that can requisition buildings and bring in the army to convert them to wards, even if the Nightingale hospitals – among the greatest achievements of the NHS during the crisis – then sit empty; spare capacity that was never needed.

An NHS, or something like it, is not just something that is nice, something that affirms a part of our national character – although it can be that. It is also a pragmatic economic necessity; a healthy nation ensures the health of all. And if, perhaps as you draw a rainbow on the pavement, it gives you a warm and cosy – possibly even slightly smug and superior – feeling, then you have missed the obvious corollary. Health and viruses do not stop at our borders. We in the UK might have universal healthcare, but the world does not. 'This is a matter of basic human solidarity. It is also crucial for combating the virus,' said António Guterres, the UN secretary-general, calling for more funding for global health[2]. 'The worst thing that could happen is to suppress the disease in developed countries and let it spread like fire in the developing world.' There it would remain – a permanent reservoir waiting to reinfect the richer world.

When this is all over there will be a reckoning. There will be a Bretton Woods for a post-pandemic age. Many topics will be discussed – animal husbandry, mechanisms of travel restrictions, economic recovery. Another topic for discussion will be support for the developing world's health systems: how can we ensure that their response to the next pandemic is as nimble and as well resourced as ours? We should do this not because it's the right thing to do (although it is). We should do it to support an argument as true now as when the NHS was created in 1948. Their health is our health. This is a virus that spreads from human to human, with barely a thought as to what's in their wallet or their passport. In other words, we should set up a properly funded pandemic response system because doing so is in everybody's enlightened self-interest. Then, next time, we can draw pavement rainbows to the Global Health Service as well.

Notes

1. *In Place of Fear*, p. 100
2. https://www.un.org/press/en/2020/sgsm20021.doc.htm
    United Nations press release 'Secretary-General Announces $2 Billion Humanitarian Response Plan to Help "Ultra-Vulnerable" Combat COVID-19 Pandemic', 25 March 2020

WHO IS VALUED?

LINDSAY DODGSON

We might look back on the coronavirus pandemic as time where everyone, whether they are a rich celebrity, a stay-at-home parent or an office worker, learned how to live a little differently.

Drew Barrymore, now just another human living through a global crisis, candidly shared how challenging it was to be homeschooling her daughters Olive and Frankie. She told the *Today Show* she had never before felt so much respect for teachers. 'I don't know if there are good days and bad days. I think there are good hours and bad hours. I cried every day, all day long,' she said. 'It was like every church and state, it was the messiest plate I've ever held in my life. I had to be the teacher, the parent, the disciplinarian, the caretaker.'[1]

We are all very much aware of the people who we used to take for granted, such as teachers, cleaners, and all the key workers who are risking their lives for us every day. Whether they are refuse collectors, doctors, nurses, carers or supermarket workers, there's a growing consensus that these are the people we should have been appreciating all along. It is the people testing us for Covid-19 and stacking shelves who are now seen as the real heroes, rather than those we have previously labelled with any other traditional means of being 'successful', such as celebrities and business owners.

Nerys Hughes, the founder and clinical director of Whole Child Therapy, thinks children who are currently in their formative years are learning lessons during this time that they will then carry throughout their lives. 'Suddenly our bin men are worth more to us as a community, our delivery drivers mean more to us as a community, than any social media star,' she says. 'When our doctors and nurses are out there dying, and our bin men are still collecting our rubbish even though it puts them at risk, you know there's an equaliser here.'

Hughes says she's enjoying the trend that's got us realising what a human's actual value is. Her children, for example, have switched their attention from YouTube stars to David Attenborough's geography classes. 'It's interesting to see that they've run out of watching snappy YouTube videos, which they would have begged for pre-lockdown,' she says. 'Now they're like, "Please can we watch David Attenborough on the BBC and do some geography?"'

There's something to be said for going back to basics, with children finding new joy in pragmatic things like being given little jobs around the house. 'Over the last few years our children have been pumped full of gadgets and toys,' says Hughes. 'And now we're sat at home with pens and paper, and baking a cake. My son started doing some videoing himself, cooking dinners for YouTube, because he thinks that's more helpful than talking about computer games at the minute.'

With no new movies being made or high-profile events to attend, the revel and adoration of celebrities has been put on hold. There even seems to be a growing conversation to hold them to a higher standard. For example, there's been talk about how 'out of touch' some celebs have been. Gal Gadot's 'Imagine' video montage is a good example – nobody really wanted to see millionaires singing about togetherness from their expansive mansions.

Entrepreneurs who also fail to meet higher expectations are being publicly scorned, perhaps more than they would have been before. Richard Branson asked for a £500 million bailout loan from the UK government for Virgin Airlines[2] and was met with nationwide flak about his status as a self-described 'tax exile' (albeit that he maintains he didn't leave the UK for tax reasons), his ownership of a Caribbean island and a lawsuit by his company Virgin Care against the NHS. He subsequently pledged to mortgage the island[3] and cut 3000 jobs.[4]

Hughes believes this trend of demolishing the perceived value of the rich and famous will be hugely impactful for younger generations. 'I think those young pre-teens and teens are going to have a very different opinion of what it is to be valuable and what it is to be meaningful,' she says, 'and we all strive for that. It's an innate human joy, isn't it? To strive to be valued and to be meaningful and to be important to people.'

In the past few years, a great deal of perceived value has been given to superficial things such as Instagram followers, with people conflating their worth with what their social-media stats say. Hughes thinks this idea may have started imploding on itself even before the pandemic, with more reality stars opening up about the mental-health toll of being an online influencer. The harsh criticism, trolling and constant pressure to stay relevant brings anxieties and depression for some, with some of the most tragic recent cases ending in suicide.[5]

The lockdown and coronavirus may just have been a reason for 'that friction to be reflected upon', Hughes says. 'I think if you look through history, there are always critical points that become catalyst for change. As the human race, we've never had disasters or wars or crises that haven't enabled us to progress and evolve.' Hughes says it's a little as though humanity's norm for what is important has been burned down and it's time something new rises from the ashes.

Maybe the ripple effect of the tragedies we've seen during this pandemic could be a re-evaluation of what really matters. We might go forward as a society with a profound sense of respect for those doing the day-to-day jobs, realising the true value of habitual things we once took for granted and leading us to become more thoughtful and compassionate overall.

Notes

1. https://www.instagram.com/tv/B-90aWxDhuA/
2. https://www.theguardian.com/business/2020/apr/12/
richard-branson-facing-backlash-over-plea-for-uk-bailout-of-virgin

   Neate, R., 'Richard Branson Facing Backlash Over Plea for UK Bailout of Virgin', *Guardian*, 12 April 2020
3. https://www.theguardian.com/business/2020/apr/20/
richard-branson-renews-virgin-plea-for-coronavirus-support

   Neate, R., 'Branson to Mortgage Caribbean Island As He Seeks Virgin Bailout', *Guardian*, 20 April 2020
4. https://www.telegraph.co.uk/business/2020/05/05/
virgin-atlantic-cuts-3000-jobs-ends-gatwick-flights/

   Gill, O., 'Virgin Atlantic Cuts 3,000 Jobs and Ends Gatwick Flights', *Telegraph*, 5 May 2020
5. https://www.insider.com/
toxic-tragic-results-of-online-hate-bullying-cancel-culture-2020-2

   Dodgson, L., 'The Frenzy of Unrelenting Online Bullying Further Destroys the Mental Health of Those Already Suffering, and Everyone Has a Role to Play', *Insider*, 25 February 2020

READING

LUCY MANGAN

You know you must be living in interesting times when both Dean Koontz and Albert Camus are racing up the bestseller lists. Ebook sales of Koontz's *The Eyes of Darkness*[1] jumped by 3000 per cent after a picture of an apparently prophetic page of his 1989 tome started doing the rounds on social media. It told of a lethal virus known as Wuhan-400 emerging from the Chinese province and sweeping the world, and there was just something about it that struck a chord . . .

The increased interest in Camus' 1947 classic *La Peste* – *The Plague* – was perhaps more predictable. The portrait of a community in lockdown as a rat-borne pestilence invades their unassuming little town normally sells around 200 copies a month in the UK. In the first three weeks of lockdown it sold ten times that. Second World War and Nazi allegory it might be, but ignore that fancy-dan stuff and it also functions as a pretty useful psychological roadmap when you find yourself in almost exactly the same plague-stricken circumstance in real life.

In times of crisis we turn to books, to art, to drama, to

music, to film or television – to any work by people who have already traversed strange terrains and maelstroms of new feelings in fact or in imagination, who can put words (or in music's case, something more extraordinary) to the ineffable, and have started to render them explicable and manageable for us.

Much of what follows is about books rather than other forms of art. This is partly because they are what I turn to most instinctively for company, for guidance, for succour and escapism where others might turn to opera or exhibitions (online – now wash your hands); and partly because, as the cultural emanation (initially at least) most unaffected and unchanged by pandemic conditions (a book requires only that you take it down from a shelf – you don't have to go out, use public transport, sit in an audience or rely on another group of people's ability to attend rehearsals and stay fit and healthy enough to be there on the night; you don't even have to fight over the remote), they are what people turned to first and, maybe, most enduringly.

In the first few weeks of lockdown, newspapers, websites, Twitter and Facebook filled with lists and recommendations for reading that were filtered through every possible prism, catering to every possible taste. Dystopian fiction for those who really wanted to lean in. Crime novels and thrillers for those who needed worlds where problems were solved and justice done. Light comedy or commercial fiction for those who (hi!) no longer had the bandwidth to marvel at exquisite sentence structure or fight their way through pages trailing clouds of literary glory. Comfort reading, aspirational reading (I started *War and Peace* before realising that this was absolutely not the time to be starting *War and Peace* because the Battle of Austerlitz pales in comparison to trying to home-school a recalcitrant eight-year-old in the guest bedroom every morning) and all points in between – browse any curation and take your pick.

After nearly seven weeks of lockdown, a study by Nielsen Book found that 41 per cent of adults were reading more (51 per cent because they had more spare time, 51 per cent because they wanted to be entertained, 35 per cent because they 'wanted escape from the crisis') and that the average time spent reading had increased from three and a half hours a week to six.

The irony, of course, was that just as books became perfectly placed to be the great beneficiaries of the apocalypse and a captive audience, practical barriers were thrown up as first bookshops lost customers, then had to close (independents first, and then chains), then further up the supply chain things ground to a halt, too. Wholesalers withdrew while they figured out new, safe working practices. Amazon deemed books to fall outside the 'essential' products they started prioritising for delivery and, for a time, seemed to have stopped taking further orders for books for their warehouses. And publishers (all figuring out ways to work remotely themselves) postponed planned publications so authors and titles didn't get lost in the chaos.

Not ideal – especially for independent publishers, who, despite finding various innovative ways of getting books out to customers and busting their asses (technical term) to do so, are suffering falls in income that makes many business futures look uncertain. But … But. There is also the possibility that what we have here is more of an opportunity for books and the book trade than it initially seems.

On the practical side, the situation may provide the impetus many have felt publishers have long needed to shake up a business model that was forged in the 1920s and hasn't much changed in response to vastly different circumstances (even pre-Covid) since. It has exposed their dependence on Amazon and may fuel a fightback against the near-monopoly of the e-retailer that has so far lacked the requisite fire. (In a more minor key, the same may also be true of customers who experienced for the first time their vulnerability to Bezos's whims. It ain't essential unless he says it's essential, remember?) And at least one publisher has noted that working remotely has proved an overall success (as it has to many employers in various industries not hitherto in favour), which means there is even less justification now for a non-diverse workforce in publishing; once you lessen the need for access to London or other capital-city offices, you open yourself up to a much broader socio-economic range of applicants, which can break a number of hegemonies.

Among the less tangible benefits, we might number the hope that Nielsen Book's recorded increase in reading time is not just a result of bookworms retreating ever more comprehensively into their protected places, but of Corona Times having given birth to new readers, pushing those who wouldn't naturally – under normal, endlessly distracting, multiple-platformed conditions – pick up a book into doing so. Boredom is a powerful impetus to try new things, and we shouldn't be too proud to take advantage of this or to build on it.

There's a fact that when a growing need – whether among old hands or bright-eyed new fans – for something meets a limited supply of it, a new appreciation is born. Perhaps the lockdown weeks will serve as a warning shot across the bows of readers beyond the pathologically dedicated few who, like me, habitually lie awake worrying about what would happen if books suddenly somehow disappeared (or, less flippantly and far more frighteningly, blindness descended) about the fragility of the book ecosystem and prompt changes in our behaviour accordingly.

Perhaps, in short, it will give us – for books and any other form of art – a way of realising what we have before it's gone. And making sure we keep it instead. Now, if you will excuse me, I've got some Koontz to buy.

Notes

1.   Headline, 2012 (ebook version)

HOW CORONAVIRUS COULD MAKE US HEALTHIER

SARAH KNAPTON

Towards the end of April, scientists at Oxford University made a curious discovery.

Despite thousands of people dying from coronavirus, the overall death rate from respiratory infections was noticeably lower than usual.

Carl Heneghan, Professor of Evidence-Based Medicine at Oxford, concluded that the lockdown was having an unexpected effect on health. Not only was it preventing the spread of coronavirus, but lack of contact between people was stifling the usual spread of other potentially lethal infectious diseases, such as influenza and viral pneumonia, which together account for around 35-40,000 deaths each year.[1]

During the week of 17 April 2019, around 15 per cent of all deaths were respiratory, but that nearly halved this year as the country stayed inside, meticulously washed their hands and observed a strict two-metre separation.

Although coronavirus, social distancing, lockdown and economic strife undoubtedly played havoc with the population's physical and mental health, in some circumstances well-being actually improved.

The major drop in pollution for several months, brought on by dramatic falls in road, rail and air travel, is likely to have had a major impact on public health. There are an estimated 40,000 deaths in the UK per year linked to outdoor air pollution, and four million worldwide, with dirty air linked to lung cancer, stroke, heart disease, Alzheimer's and fatal asthma. The government's Committee on the Medical Effects of Air Pollutants has concluded that a yearly rise of 10 micrograms in average levels of fine particulates causes a 6 per cent uptick in mortality[2]. To put that in context, Port Talbot, the area in the UK with the highest levels of particulates, due to its heavy steel industry, records an average level of 18 micrograms, nearly double the World Health Organization (WHO) recommendation of 10 micrograms or below.

But during the months of lockdown, pollution fell by more than 50 per cent in some areas, and some experts even speculated that such huge improvements may be large enough to offset some of the mortality from coronavirus. Dr Marshall Burke, a professor of Earth System Science at Stanford University, calculated that the reduction in particulate matter from the Chinese lockdown probably saved the lives of 4000 young children and 73,000 elderly adults in the country this year.[2] Although Burke said it was foolhardy to think pandemics could be good for health, he did accept it was a useful reminder of the often-hidden health consequences of 'life as usual'.

Not only was pollution lower when people were outside, but overall exposure was less because people were no longer walking on the streets.

The Centre for Research on Energy and Clean Air suggested that the UK's coronavirus lockdown, coupled with ongoing falls in coal-powered electricity generation, will save as many as 3425 lives due to less air pollution in 2020. For Europe as a whole, it could be as many as 11,000 lives.

The Norwegian Institute for Nature Research also found that during just two weeks of lockdown the number of cases of asthma in children reduced by 6600 across 27 countries where the measures were in force.[3]

In China and India, lockdown is thought to have saved 1400 and 5300 respectively from premature mortality due to particulates in just a fortnight. And they predicted that if lockdown lasted all year, it would save 780,000 lives globally from pollution, far more than the number that died from coronavirus.

Research by Harvard University also suggests people were more at risk from contracting coronavirus in more polluted areas, so inadvertently cleaning up the air may have had the unforeseen benefit of lowering the number of cases, particularly in deprived areas.[4]

Likewise, the fall in noise pollution has undoubtedly been beneficial to health, as the perpetual roar of traffic died away in cities and was replaced by birdsong and rustling leaves. According to WHO, noise pollution affects more than 100 million people across Europe and is responsible for premature death equivalent to around 1.6 million healthy years of life each year. Harvard researchers from the 'Noise and the City' programme have seen rush-hour noise levels drop by two thirds in areas of Boston during lockdown.[5]

In 2017, researchers from Nottingham Trent University found that the cacophony of noise in town centres can trigger heart problems. The team found that it is not just the level of noise that is a problem, but also the constant change to that noise. Urbanites are subjected to an anxiety-inducing symphony of slamming doors, car horns, sirens and building work, which has an immediate and disruptive effect on the patterns of normal heart rates. Other research has linked noise pollution to high blood pressure, sleep disruption and stress disorders. It can also impact the circadian rhythm, which is crucial to good health.[6]

So several months of quieter conditions was good for the mind and body. Working from home also brought surprising benefits. Absolved of the torturous daily commute and no longer required to get their children ready for school, workers were able to get far more sleep, and were no longer enslaved to their alarms, allowing natural rhythms to reset.

Even a little more sleep can have huge benefits to health, boosting the immune system, improving attention and concentration, helping maintain a healthy weight and protecting mental health.

With the shutdown of restaurants and concerns about catching coronavirus from takeaway delivery services, the diets of Britons also began to improve. Social media was awash with people trying new home-cooked recipes, while the supermarket queues suddenly made everyday shopping items seem like prized possessions. After the initial panic-buying cleared the shelves of long-lasting processed foods, shoppers had no choice but to turn to fresher and healthier ingredients.

The closure of bars and pubs also had a noticeable impact as A & E units, normally crammed with drinkers on Friday and Saturday nights, fell quiet.

Extra time, and being allowed outside only to exercise, meant that people upped their exercise routines, and thousands of instructors moved their businesses online, giving people no excuse to miss their sessions. And without cleaners, people who had not picked up a mop in years were forced to put in more effort to keep their homes sparkling.

The show of solidarity during the pandemic was also good for health, according to experts. Within twenty-four hours of the government calling for volunteers to help with the crisis, an 'army' of 500,000 Britons had signed up to deliver medication, drive patients to appointments and make phone calls to those in isolation. By early April, volunteer numbers had risen beyond 750,000.

Many people said they had joined up to address the sad situations they were hearing about and to feel they were doing something to help. But it was also hugely beneficial to them, researchers believe. A sense of solidarity is known to overcome feelings of helplessness while boosting self-esteem, counteracting low mood, reducing anxiety and producing more positive thinking. It also boosts social capital, increasing the number of resources and contacts that people can turn to for assistance, an important metric that is linked to how long people live.

If nothing else, lockdown has shown what a cleaner, greener world would look like, demonstrated how illness can be stopped through good hygiene and revealed just how many lives could be spared and improved by decarbonising the planet.

The virus been a tragedy to many, but the response to it has also been an astonishing natural experiment and, ironically, it may end up ushering in a new era of fresher air, healthier populations and less disease.

Notes

1. https://www.cebm.net/covid-19/tracking-mortality-over-time/

    Oke, J., DeVito, N., Henegan, C. 'Tracking Mortality over Time', The Centre for Evidence-Based Medicine, 3 April 2020. Data for England and Wales only.

2. https://assets.publishing.service.gov.uk/government/uploads/system/uploads/attachment_data/file/304641/COMEAP_mortality_effects_of_long_term_exposure.pdf

3. http://www.g-feed.com/2020/03/covid-19-reduces-economic-activity.html

    Burke, M., 'COVID-19 Reduces Economic Activity, Which Reduces Pollution, Which Saves Lives', G-Feed, 8 March 2020.

4. https://www.medrxiv.org/content/10.1101/2020.04.10.20060673v1

    Venter, Z.S., Aunan, K., Chowdhury, S., Lelieveld, J., 'COVID-19 Lockdowns Cause Global Air Pollution Declines With Implications For Public Health Risk' Medrxiv.org, 14 April 2020.

5. https://www.hsph.harvard.edu/news/hsph-in-the-news/air-pollution-linked-with-higher-covid-19-death-rates/

    Harvard T.H. Chan School of Public Heath, article updated 5 May 2020.

6.   http://noiseandthecity.org/about-noise-and-the-city/

7.   https://www.telegraph.co.uk/science/2017/06/24/noisy-cities-disrupt-heartbeat-could-trigger-disease-study-suggests/

  Knapton, S., 'Noisy Cities Disrupt Heartbeat And Could Trigger Disease, Study Suggests' *Telegraph*, 25 June 2017

ABSENCE MAKES THE HEART GROW STRONGER

LINDSAY DODGSON

I was never really much of a phone call person before the lockdown. I talk on the phone so much for my job as a journalist, it just wasn't something I wanted to do very much when I got home.

But now I am finding video calls an immense comfort as a way to stay connected to the people I care about, and I'm building new avenues of friendships with the ones I already considered myself to be very close to. I'd hazard a guess that many of you are feeling the same.

This is a novel opportunity to work out who in your friendship and family circles is the most important to you – accidentally or otherwise. For instance, you might be finding you are talking to some people more than ever, while you just don't have the enthusiasm for other conversations.

Trauma therapist Shannon Thomas, author of *Healing from Hidden Abuse: A Journey Through the Stages of Recovery from Psychological Abuse*[1], says the coronavirus pandemic is a 'slow-moving disaster' where we can't always expect to have the capacity for engaging emotionally. 'We're collectively exhausted, and with that experience we will not have the energy to keep in touch with each person who might expect to hear from us,' she says. 'If we find ourselves feeling guilty for not reaching out to certain people, it's helpful to remember that we're attempting to get through each and every long day as best we can.'

Thomas says it's a matter of taking our emotional vitals each day and working out what our needs are, rather than defining our worth from someone else's expectations. This is why some relationships will thrive and others will fizzle out.

Judith Orloff, author of *The Empath's Survival Guide: Life Strategies for Sensitive People*[2], says distance is a great equaliser in this way, and we should treasure that clarity. 'It gives us the perspective to see people clearly when perhaps we didn't before,' she says. 'You might realise how much you really love and treasure someone – and thus want to increase contact when the time comes.'

According to research, absence really does make the heart grow stronger. A study in the *Journal of Communication*, published in 2013,[3] found that long-distance relationships could be more intimate, trusting and satisfying because the rare interactions between couples were more meaningful. Being apart also helped long-distance couples think of their partner in a more idealistic way. So, all that longing for someone, whether it's your romantic partner or your friends, is probably going to be worth it because it'll make your connection stronger.

On the other hand, some of us might be noticing there are certain people we don't want to be in contact with any more at all. In China, for instance, there was a spike in divorce rates after couples emerged from weeks of quarantining together,[4] and domestic violence cases are on the rise all over the world as more people are stuck inside with someone who's abusive.[5]

According to psychologist Perpetua Neo, who works with women who are recovering from abusive relationships, this is a time when toxic dynamics might reveal themselves more clearly. Abusive partners 'need to appear really charming in public,' Neo says, 'but they can only use up a certain amount of energy before they have to melt down and be their real self.'

Shannon Thomas says we may have quietly adopted coping skills to help us deal with the other person's toxicity, but isolation means the ability to implement these is abruptly removed. 'It removes the daily routine that helped dilute the intensity of other people's behaviours,' she says.

Signs of a toxic relationship include feeling trapped or as though you're always walking on eggshells. Someone dismissing your feelings, always turning the blame on you or making you feel like you're going crazy are big red flags of gaslighting – where someone lies and gives a version of reality to fit their own narrative, in order to control their victim.

All of this isn't as much of a disaster as it sounds. Being thrown into turmoil from a global crisis could give people the strength to get out of bad relationships for good. It takes the average person between five and seven attempts to leave an abusive relationship, according to the Domestic Violence Prevention centre[6], so coming out of such an intense few weeks with a new perspective on a partner may mean the break-up finally sticks.

Grief is being felt on an international, collective level, and noticing toxic traits in someone will only add to that. So, if you've come to the realisation that someone is causing you physical, mental or emotional harm, you shouldn't feel guilty about cutting them out of your life for good.

It is essential that everyone is self-compassionate right now, whether or not they are going through an abusive situation. Judith Orloff says we should be constantly checking the needs of both our mental and physical health. There is no shame in turning down Zoom calls if you're feeling burned out or overwhelmed, for example, and you shouldn't feel guilty for putting your own mental health first. This doesn't mean your friendships are any less important than they were. Introverts need time to regroup and recharge after social interactions,[7] and video calls fall very much into this category. You might even find some of your friends are feeling the same way, and suddenly your conversations transform from an obligation to something that is more meaningful to you all.

'It's important to go for what relationships work for you, and feel the love,' Orloff says. 'A great lesson this lockdown has shown us is that we are all interconnected on this earth and we are one family.' Understanding this connection, and thinking about how everyone is going through the same thing, can help us feel less isolated, even if we are taking some time out to be solitary. This knowledge, Orloff says, 'can make us feel less alone and work towards emotional, social and poetical harmony, empathy and respect for all people, everywhere.'

Notes

1. Mast Publishing House, 2016
2. Sounds True Inc, 2017
3. https://cpb-us-e1.wpmucdn.com/blogs.cornell.edu/dist/c/6136/files/2014/01/2013-Jiang-Hancock-Absence-makes-the-communication-grow-fonder.pdf

    Jiang, C. L. and Hancock, J. T., 'Absence Makes the Communication Grow Fonder: Geographic Separation, Interpersonal Media, and Intimacy in Dating Relationships', Journal of Communication, 2013, Vol.63, pp.556–77
4. https://www.bloomberg.com/news/articles/2020-03-31/divorces-spike-in-china-after-coronavirus-quarantines

    Prasso, S., 'China's Divorce Spike Is a Warning to Rest of Locked-Down World', *Bloomberg Businessweek*, 31 March 2020
5. https://www.businessinsider.com/as-the-coronavirus-pandemic-grows-so-does-domestic-violence-2020-4?r=US&IR=T

    Al-Arshani, S., '9 Large Metro Police Departments Reported "Double-Digit Percentage Jumps" in Domestic Violence 911 Calls As More People Shelter At Home', *Business Insider*, 7 April 2020
6. https://www.domesticviolence.com.au/files/pdf/Info-Book-Final.pdf

7. https://www.businessinsider.com/
    what-is-an-introvert-hangover-2018-5
        Dodgson, L., 'Here's How to Tell If You're Experiencing an
    "Introvert Hangover"', *Business Insider*, 20 Ma 2018

PANGOLIN

TOM WHIPPLE

The pangolin's scales are meant to be there for its protection. They are the armour behind which it can retreat, safe from a world that has never considered this creature to be among its beauties or wonders.

Not that the pangolin ever wanted to be noticed. Until recently, it lived a simple life. After evolution made the pangolin, it saw little need to improve it. For more than 50 million years, the pangolin and its ancestors have looked much the same and lived in much the same way, snuffling their snouts into the termite and ant mounds of the tropics (the scaly ant-eater – the pangolin's other name – is voracious, consuming 20,000 of the insects a day). For all those years, the armour did its job. If an animal approached looking for lunch, the pangolin just snapped into an impregnable sphere, curled up in a ball of keratin, and the predator quickly gave up and left it alone.

But then, just a few pangolin-generations ago, the protective scales became a liability. They were, some humans claimed, good at warding off disease. They could speed up lactation; they could cure palsy. In Vietnam, they were even included on some health insurance plans. Now, when the pangolin curled into a ball, these humans came along and just picked it up.

Until the pandemic, few people cared about the pangolin. They cared about its scales, yes. And they cared about its meat – exotic meat caters to exotic tastes. But they didn't care about it as an animal in its own right. Instead, like many endangered species, the pangolin bumped along the bottom of the world's conservation priorities, protected in principle but not in practice. Despite supposedly having the strongest of legal prohibitions, 100,000 pangolins a year were snatched from the wild and taken to market.

Then came the law no one can evade: karma. Scientists think that one of those scaly balls that got picked up may have contained an invisible package of replicating protein – better known as a virus – that would make this apparently lucrative trade the costliest in history. A pangolin, they believe, had caught coronavirus from a bat, and somewhere in a Chinese live-animal market it was about to give it to a human. And suddenly, we all cared. Suddenly the pangolin, and animals like it, had a new and compelling argument in favour of their protection.

Conservationists refer to some animals as 'charismatic'. These are the animals that appear on posters and in Pixar movies. They are the rhinos and elephants, the pandas and tigers. Most animals, though, are not charismatic. Especially if they are brown, small, eat ants and look a bit like a stretchy artichoke with legs.

For these Cinderella species, the species that never find their way into conservation logos or wildlife photography exhibitions, extinction comes with not a bang but a whimper. Across the world, animals are killed for meat or for medicine. More often, they die as mere collateral: their habitats are destroyed, forcing them into the encroaching towns and cities, where they cannot survive. Gradually, inexorably, they creep towards extinction.

If an animal dies in a forest, and no one knew its name, did it ever exist? The answer is if a virus in that animal manages to use it to infect the world, people learn its name pretty fast.

From this answer, counter-intuitively, comes hope.

We will never know for certain what happened in Wuhan – and as more evidence is collected, competing theories have emerged. But here is the most popular guess. A coronavirus had passed among bats, which, like humans, live close together in large colonies. For the bats, this infection would probably have been mild – a bat cold. After all, a virus has no interest in killing its host: it needs the living in order to reproduce.

One day, a single mutation in the virus caused it to jump into another animal – quite probably a pangolin. Then that pangolin found itself in a live animal market. Here, it brushed alongside other animals. There were cats in cages and dogs in baskets. There were rats, snakes and lizards, squirrels, foxes, civets and turtles. There were endangered animals and domestic animals. All came together in a great melee, to be inspected by humans – themselves packed almost as tightly.

Nothing about this especially troubled the world until the start of 2020. Now these circumstances, and the trade in animals everywhere, trouble the world greatly. A study published in early April, on the same day that Britain's prime minister went into intensive care to be treated for coronavirus, looked at where human diseases come from; which factors determine which animals give us diseases. It found, not surprisingly, that, historically, many human diseases come from domesticated animals. These are the animals that we spend most time around, and which – in the case of chickens and pigs – we pack tightest together. But we already have many of their diseases. There was, the researchers found, another category, which is plentiful and unpredictable: quite literally, a wild card.

The animals in this category were the ones of which humans have little experience but into whose lives we increasingly encroach. These are the animals we hunt and capture, and whose territories we invade. They are the primates that gave us Ebola, Zika virus and HIV, the wild migrating birds that spread influenza; they are the bats behind henipavirus, the wallabies behind Ross River fever, the sparrows behind psittacosis.

They are the animals we have no business being with. Or, as David Quammen, author of *Spillover: Animal Infections and the Next Human Pandemic*[1], wrote: 'We invade tropical forests and other wild landscapes, which harbor so many species of animals and plants – and within those creatures, so many unknown viruses. We cut the trees; we kill the animals or cage them and send them to markets. We disrupt ecosystems, and we shake viruses loose from their natural hosts. When that happens, they need a new host. Often, we are it.'

China has announced an immediate ban on the trading and eating of many wild animals, including pangolins. Wuhan has gone further, banning the eating, breeding and hunting of all wild animals. On World Pangolin Day, never normally a highlight of the annual calendar, the Chinese Communist Party appealed for pangolin love. It may be that, eventually, we find out the pangolin had nothing to do with this at all. It no longer really matters – the fact that it could have been responsible is enough.

The world knows it cannot go back to its previous ways after this pandemic, to the days where an animal worth a few hundred pounds per kilogram could cause a few trillion pounds of destruction. The conclusion is simple. It is the cry of ugly animals everywhere: if we can't save these animals for their sakes, maybe we can do it for our own.

TALKING MENTAL HEALTH

LINDSAY DODGSON

How many times a day do you ask someone how they are? How many times do you hear the question in return? It was probably countless back in the days of normal social contact – so many, perhaps, that half the time you barely noticed.

Psychologist and emotional intelligence pioneer Marc Brackett holds up a mirror to this habitual cycle of ours in his book *Permission to Feel: Unlocking the Power of Emotions to Help Our Kids, Ourselves and Our Society Thrive*[2], where he calls it a 'paradox of the human condition'. Why do we ask, he says, if we never 'expect or desire – or provide – an honest answer'?

There are probably just as many 'how are you's in our new lockdown world, in the form of WhatsApp messages, video calls and emails. But you might be finding that you're spending a little more time actually thinking about it and really answering that question. It could be more willingness to speak openly about how you're anxious about what's going on in the world. Or you might tell your friends about the waves of depression that are making it hard to get out of bed in the morning to spend another day working from home. These admissions, however small, bring us closer to each other and are steps towards breaking down the stigma that has surrounded mental health for so long.

A recent survey from the Academy of Medical Sciences[3] found five overarching mental health themes that are concerning the public during the coronavirus pandemic: anxiety, isolation and loneliness, developing a mental illness, finding access to the right help, and worries about their friends and family.

It's a tremendously hard time for people who have mental health problems, with the charity Mind saying it's already difficult for everyone to access the support they need.[4] There are also concerns from psychologists and therapists that the worsening of mental illnesses could persist for years after the pandemic is over.[5]

The silver lining may be the global conversation changing just enough for us to keep talking about mental health in the right way and for more people get the help they need. Chris Boutté, a YouTuber and mental health advocate who has worked as an addiction specialist, says he would like to see people no longer tiptoeing around discussions about depression and anxiety. He also hopes international lockdowns are getting people talking to each other, rather than relying on social media. 'I think a lot of people are becoming accustomed to blasting out to the internet instead of having conversations,' he says. 'Because there's a difference between me reaching out to you personally and being like, "Hey, I'm struggling right now – here are some thoughts I'm having, here are some emotions I'm having," and going on Twitter and saying, "Life sucks; everything's terrible."'

Speaking one-on-one, whether it's in person or through messaging, gets the thoughts out of your head and into the world. Writing them as a public Facebook status or a tweet isn't as effective, and just keeps those thoughts spinning around in your vicinity. All the kind responses give you validation that soon fades away, as any addiction does. If you get no responses at all, it's even worse. 'What I'm hoping is more people, since they're stuck in the house together, are having those conversations with each other,' Boutté says.

Before the coronavirus pandemic, so many of us were always in a rush, telling each other we were 'fine' while simultaneously tackling any number of internal battles. We've now been forced to slow down and have some quietness in our lives, which can be disconcerting if you're used to giving yourself a busy schedule to avoid being too introspective.

For some people the fear of Covid-19 may be enough for them to start feeling overwhelmed and buried, and to seek mental-health help. But others are reaching out because things they never realised they were pushing down have finally reached the surface. It's only through therapy that it can become clear that worries over the coronavirus have just been the catalyst for a lifetime of other anxieties bubbling over, and the root causes – whether it be childhood trauma, career stress or relationship troubles – were there all along.

Mental health professionals have seen a significant increase in people requesting their services in the last few weeks. According to a Member Feedback Survey by the British Association for Counselling and Psychotherapy[6], 26 per cent of therapists said the mental health impact of coronavirus was a key reason why people are turning to therapy, with 5.2 per cent seeing an increase in new clients since the start of lockdown.

Online therapy services such as Talkspace, Brightside and Kara Connect have seen an increase in clients of as much as 65 per cent since lockdown began,[7] and there has been a mental health start-up boom as people look for more bite-size help from apps.[8]

Kara Connect's founder, Thorbjorg Helga Vigfusdottir, says this increased access will see more people asking for help, and this might be a trend that continues when therapists open their physical doors again.

Not only has research suggested that therapy via video call can be just as effective as sessions in person,[9] it has indicated that taking it online can also be preferable for the patient. Around 25 per cent of the world's population seek help for mental health problems[10] but only about a quarter of those receive the right help. Feeling that a session was a waste of time may lead to those people never trying again. Virtual sessions are a low-stakes way of trying out therapy and possibly sticking with it a little longer.

Another trend that could continue for the better could be the mental health benefits of the humble walk. Data from Sport England's *Covid-19 Briefing*[11] suggests 63 per cent of people are exercising to help manage their mental health during the outbreak, with walking accounting for about 60 per cent of all activity.

Mindfulness trainer Karen Liebenguth says a walk is a fast-track way to relax because it slows down our minds and helps lower the heart rate, blood pressure and stress-hormone levels. 'As the body softens, the nervous system calms down and we feel more relaxed, grounded, calm and more confident about ourselves and life,' she says. 'As we let go of some of the thoughts racing in our heads, the unconscious mind stream-lines thoughts, reflects and generates new ways of thinking, ideas and solutions.'

Walking therapist Carmen Rendell says walking helps with two things that people are battling with right now: fear and grief. 'Walking helps process grief,' she says. 'It helps it flow through, rather than just sitting with it. It's free and it's ancient, and we've been doing it for centuries.'

Rendell also hopes this trend might have a positive impact on how we structure our days when offices and workplaces open up again. As many as 65 per cent of people in the US eat lunch at their desks, often after a quick dash to the supermarket for a sandwich.[12] There could be a major positive impact on everyone's mental health if they took an hour out of their day for a stroll. Karen Liebenguth says, 'I think many people will continue walking because they have formed a healthy habit. What's more, many will have experienced the beneficial impact of walking on their mental and physical well-being over several weeks now, which will motivate them to do more, to continue, to try new walks, to explore new places. The reasons for continuing walking will only grow.'

In the midst of this global crisis, the little adjustments that keep us grounded grow a new importance. Being kind to ourselves by slowing down, and extending that spirit to others, is extremely valuable to our mental state. This kindness may be in realising you don't need to learn a new skill in lockdown, or that it's okay to not be okay. Or it may simply be in finding the time to be candid with your loved ones – letting them know how you really are and lending a sincere ear in return.

Notes

1. Vintage, 2013
2. Macmillan USA, 2019
3. https://acmedsci.ac.uk/file-download/99436893

    Cowan, K. (collator), 'Understanding People's Concerns About the Mental Health Impacts of the Covid-19 Epidemic', MQ: Transforming Mental Health and the Academy of Medical Sciences, April 2020
4. https://www.bbc.co.uk/news/health-52295894

    Roxby, P., 'Coronavirus: "Profound" Mental Health Impact Prompts Calls for Urgent Research, BBC News, 16 April 2020
5. https://metro.co.uk/2020/04/10/life-coronavirus-lockdown-devastating-impact-mental-health-12539433

    Scott, E. 'Life in a Coronavirus Lockdown "Could Have a Devastating Impact on Mental Health"', *Metro*, 10 April 2020
6. https://www.bacp.co.uk/news/news-from-bacp/coronavirus/coronavirus-updates/preliminary-results-of-our-member-survey/
7. https://www.forbes.com/sites/carlieporterfield/2020/04/02/coronavirus-36-of-americans-say-pandemic-has-made-a-serious-impact-on-their-mental-health

    Porterfield, C., 'Coronavirus: 36% of Americans Say Pandemic Has Made a "Serious Impact" on Their Mental Health, *Forbes*, 2 April 2020

8. https://sifted.eu/articles/
mental-health-startups-are-in-high-demand-these-days/
    Gillet, K., 'Mental Health Startups Boom As Pandemic Anxieties Worsen', *Sifted*, 13 April 2020

9. https://www.apa.org/monitor/2017/02/online-therapy
    Novotney, A., 'A Growing Wave of Online Therapy', Monitor on Psychology, *American Psychological Association*, February 2017, Vol.47(2), p.48

10. https://www.who.int/whr/2001/media_centre/press_release/en/
    'Mental Disorders Affect One in Four People', *World Health Report 2001*, World Health Organization, 2001

11. 'Covid-19 Briefing: Exploring Attitudes and Behaviours in England During the Covid-19 Pandemic', Sport England, April 2020

12. https://www.tricitymed.org/2017/05/sad-desk-lunch-infographic/
    'The Sad Desk Lunch', Tri-City Medical Center, www.tricitymed.org

LONG-DISTANCE FRIENDSHIPS

ALEX HERN

I have not met up with anyone I don't live with for weeks. I can vividly remember the last weekend of the Before Times, because it was unusually busy for me. The pubs were still open, friends were still popping round to each other's homes, and I saw different groups on Friday, Saturday and Sunday. No one had planned it as a last hurrah, but there was the sense that it might be anyway; I worked from home for the following week, and the Monday after that, the prime minster announced the restrictions that would go on to dominate most of the year.

But then something funny happened, for me as well as for millions of others around the world: my social calendar started filling up. When one person is trapped at home, it's a lonely, isolating experience. When everyone is trapped at home, it's something else.

Currently, my regular commitments include coffee with two friends on Thursday mornings; a tabletop roleplaying game which I run every other Thursday evening; a board game I play with a local couple on Tuesday evenings; a regular Mario

Kart competition every Friday with a couple in Santa Clara; a catch-up with my mother, usually on Sunday evenings; a crafts session during weekend daytimes; and another tabletop roleplaying game which I play on Wednesday evenings, which somehow clashes with drinks with my colleagues at the same time. All, of course, are carried out over video chats. And yes, the substance of my calendar skews to the nerdy end, but the scale of it is the new normal.

Webcams lie at the heart of a lot of this. We know, instinctively, how important it is to see and interact with others in lockdown. Traditional social media are the empty calories of human interaction, filling your surface desire to know what's happening in the lives of your friends and loved ones, but providing little of the feeling of actually hanging out with them. And so the first few weeks of isolation saw those of us with access to professional videoconferencing tools spreading the wisdom: first with everyone using whatever they could get their hands on, then with Zoom emerging as the crossover hit before Microsoft and Google improved their own free offerings to try to stem the flow of users.

A video-chat session can be strangely exhausting as well, though. The act of appearing to pay attention takes more effort than simply paying attention; keeping cameras trained on your face can backfire if you're looking to relax with friends. Similarly, we're all still learning a new collection of social cues: how do you end a video call? What are the polite excuses you can make to hang up on a chat, when everyone knows you don't have anywhere to be and when all your other leisure activities are going to be at the same screen you're begging off?

But learning we are, and we're all doing it together. The downsides of missing a social cue are limited when everyone else is working through exactly the same process.

These difficulties have been bundled together as a new pathology: Zoom fatigue. There are real psychological reasons for the problem. As Doreen Dodgen-Magee writes in *Psychology Today*,[1] 'the constant presence of one's own image as they interact with others' brings with it a 'kind of acute self-awareness'. A persistent picture of yourself in the corner of your vision 'can have a massive impact on how one is, or is not, in the present moment of a conversation in an authentic and available way'. Dodgen-Magee recommends simply covering that preview image – literally sticking a Post-It over the corner of the screen.

Of course, much of what is being dubbed 'Zoom fatigue' is really just a symptom of the wider challenges of living in lockdown. We're exhausted because our working days have extended in both directions, or we are constantly stressing about the state of the world, and when we do sit down to relax, we often do it with the same screen, in the same chair, on the same software that we've just spent hours working on throughout the day.

Allow for those factors, though, and video calls are a net positive on many mental health metrics: a 2013 study published in the journal *Cyberpsychology*, for instance, found video chat second only to in-person meetings for bonding with others.[2] In 2018, The *American Journal of Geriatric Psychiatry* reported that 'users of video chat had approximately half the probability of depressive symptoms' compared to non-users, even if the latter used email, social media and instant messaging to stay in touch.[3]

So popular are all these video chats that they're causing moderate struggles with the very infrastructure that makes up the internet. As work-from-home orders came down, there was a fear that residential internet connections might not be able to cope. Would networks collapse, leaving industries struggling to adapt?

Thankfully, the key limit for most connections isn't overall use, but peak bandwidth. The network is built to handle the period when the most people are downloading the most data simultaneously, and for residential connections, that's early evening, as Netflix and iPlayer streams are joined around the nation. The peak did cause some sweaty moments for the internet service providers, which saw an increase in use of about 15 per cent as other evening activities died off, but quick action from the video providers themselves prevented a crisis: first Netflix, then YouTube, Facebook, Amazon and Sony all took actions to reduce the quality of their videos and the speed of their downloads, helping to keep the evening peak manageable.

But the peak accounts only for download traffic: the real increase came in uploads. For the vast majority of us, the data we send out to the internet is dwarfed by the data we download from it; the occasional email or uploaded photo is nothing compared to hours of Netflix, and our connections are built with that asymmetry in mind. Once the social distancing started, though, and households around the world began spending hours each day broadcasting high-definition video of themselves to friends and loved ones, and upstream traffic almost doubled, according to Virgin Media. On WhatsApp, the typical peak for calls is New Year's Eve, when people around the world contact each other at the same time to say 'Happy New Year'. By mid March, Mark Zuckerberg told reporters earlier this year, traffic was 'on a sustained basis well beyond that spike on New Year's'.

The spike in virtual socialising has had knock-on effects. Some are around the format of such sessions: for all the technological marvel of being able to bring twenty people together for a live video chat, it can be an overwhelming experience to try and organise one. More gregarious folk than me have managed to handle the freewheeling conversations that ensue, but for others, there is appeal in something to structure the fun around, and so virtual games, activities and hobbies are seeing a boost.

At one end of that spectrum are literal video games. Everything from classic first-person shooters like *Call of Duty* to the quaint pastoral friendship-sim of *Animal Crossing* has seen a spike in use since lockdown, but this by no means reflects a corresponding growth in time spent alone. Instead, more folk than ever are using the online features in such games to find something to do with their friends beyond simply staring at each other down a camera and wishing they were together in person instead. (So much so, in fact, that all of the major online gaming services suffered outages during the first week of widespread social distancing, while several smaller ones saw their concurrent user count double or triple their previous all-time highs).

Perhaps the clearest example of a structure for hangouts is virtual role-playing. A niche hobby at the best of times, a game like *Dungeons and Dragons* is nonetheless perfectly suited to spending time with friends via webcam: in fact, all roleplaying games really are is a set of rules, some complex and some simple, for moderating a shared conversation. Many even have a role, the games master, whose job in part is to explicitly tell people when it's their turn to speak. In real life, that may be stifling for many, but in lockdown it can be a godsend.

It's not just the nerds who are adapting to the new normals of socialising, though. Take Houseparty, one of the stand-out successes of the era. The video-chat app, owned by the creators of *Fortnite*, was built for an audience of American college students wanting to hang out with old friends at other universities, before it found a new, much larger, potential user base once everyone else found themselves relying on tech for friendship, too. Houseparty has long had a selection of quick party games built into it, specifically to solve the question of what people should actually do once they find themselves on a video chat with their friends.

It would be wrong to say I'm not looking forward to the world opening up again. But I hope that when it does, I manage to continue to maintain the long-distance friendships I've rekindled: to remember that my pals in New York are always up for a lazy Saturday of board games, that my friends around the UK can be easily brought together for an evening of beers over a webcam, and that my world is larger that just the places I can get to with a zones-one-and-two travelcard between finishing work and cooking dinner at home.

Notes

1. https://www.psychologytoday.com/us/blog/deviced/202004/
    why-video-chats-are-wearing-us-out

    Dodgen-Magee, D., 'Why Video Chats Are Wearing Us Out',
    Psychology Today, 17 April 2020

2. https://doi.org/10.5817/CP2013-2-3

    Sherman, L. E. Michikyan, M., Greenfield, P. M., 'The
    Effects of Text, Audio, Video, and In-Person Communication
    on Bonding Between Friends', *Cyberpsychology*, 2013, Vol.7(2),
    Article 3

3. https://doi.org/10.1016/j.jagp.2018.10.014

    Teo, A. R., Markwardt, S. and Hinton, L., 'Using Skype to
    Beat the Blues: Longitudinal Data from a National Representative
    Sample', *The American Journal of Geriatric Psychiatry*, March 2019,
    Vol.27(3), pp.254–62

WHEN INTROVERTS RULED THE EARTH

LUCY MANGAN

Six and a half weeks. Six and a half weeks of lockdown passed before I felt even the mildest stirrings of the urge to go out or any yearning at all to see anyone other the two people – husband, eight-year-old son – I was locked down with. If anything, I considered myself – because of the constant gustatory entertainment and other demands of the husband and eight-year-old son, ever yapping at my heels – not quite isolated *enough*.

This, my friends, is what it is to be an introvert. The clinical definition is, roughly, 'someone who is drained by interaction with others'. An extrovert is one who is energised by it.

The latter outnumber the former – plus they make a lot more noise – so the world is, naturally, organised largely as they prefer it. The open-plan office, brainstorming sessions and paintballing awaydays for team bonding are emblematic of their influence at work. At home they have polluted life by inventing mother-and-baby groups, Facebook and parties of all kinds (though 'themed' and 'fancy dress' should be singled out for especial contumely at every turn).

Under pandemic conditions, however, things are different. Self-isolation and enforced working from home is an introvert's dream come true. This we can cope with, easily. Here, we can thrive, just as extroverts do in ordinary times. The ability to work independently, without the need for companionship or supervision, is better recognised for the asset it is. The ability to dominate a room and talk a good game garners fewer rewards on Zoom than it does in real life, as does projected confidence over the ability to deliver – suddenly a much more directly measurable quantity as work begins to arrive or, crucially, does not, from remote outposts on to managers' desks. When everyone is under blanket pressure, mere showmanship becomes tedious – you need spare bandwidth to enjoy it and suddenly that is being eaten up elsewhere. It's a frippery we no longer have the resources to indulge. And if there is no expertise beneath, once it is pared away … Historically undervalued skills begin to creep up the hierarchy. Humility or quietness is shown not necessarily to be a manifestation of self-doubt or lack of ability and is no longer automatically or subconsciously penalised as such.

For socially anxious people (i.e. those suffering from a mental health condition rather than unfashionable temperament), too, lockdown has been a blessing rather than a curse (absent any other Covid complications, of course). They are at home – a safe, controlled environment – and online interactions via video calls are much more manageable than the hurly-burly of real-life meetings and the aforementioned semi-satanic brainstorming sessions. The relative freedom to set one's own hours to coincide with the times when an anxious, idiosyncratic brain is at its calmest and best is a rare and valuable thing. As is the fact that there is currently no stigma attached to working in this way. It's been forced upon everyone. No individual allowances have had to be asked for or grudgingly granted. Entire staffs have simply been relocated under government orders. No guilt, no head above the parapet, no special pleading, no attention drawn to one's perceived 'failings'. The world has – for once, for once – rearranged itself around you without you having to do anything.

And this is but one manifestation of what can happen when the world around us shifts. All sorts of possibilities emerge. Pessimism becomes a positive trait – we tend to cope very well in a crisis; we've been preparing for ones that never happen all our lives. It's almost a relief when the other shoe drops. People who are used to being in control, ones who have been in positions of relative power and privilege all their lives, may find the new reality harder to bear than do those who are used to being buffeted by the vicissitudes of a life that never was arranged for their particular convenience. The lack of a playbook or precedent does not disturb what others unwittingly took to be the natural order of things, because this never was the natural order of lives lived in economic uncertainty. Disabled people, for whom confinement, perilous health, isolation and dependence on the peripatetic kindness of others are often normal – thanks to the parlous state of various service provisions upon which they should be able to depend – are mentally well-prepared for lockdown.

This in itself is hardly a roseate view: *Hey, look – some people were already suffering, and now they have company! Yay!* But what it does offer is two avenues that open up only under strange and usually forced conditions.

First, it offers empirical evidence of how often cultural problems are misattributed as the faults of individuals. You might have spent years berating yourself for not being good at your job, when actually it turns out the office setting of your job wasn't very good for you. Realising that sometimes in life it's not You, but Them, is a liberating, not to say revolutionary, thing. The dominant narrative of our times has been, in one form or another, that the poor, the sick, the disadvantaged in any way have brought it upon themselves. This is a myth, of course, that does not hold up under scrutiny, but how many of us, as we go – went – about our daily business, really took the time to do consider it? Now we don't have to. Proof stands before us, whether we are one of those benefiting from this suddenly upside-down world or are being forced to see life through the narrowed lens that others have always been required to use.

And second, it shows that change is possible. It shows

how little of what we think of as immutable institutions, power relations and structural systems these things really are. That's an acorn that can bury itself in the collective psyche now and flourish into a mighty oak in times to come.

THE REHABILITATION
OF EXPERTS

SARAH KNAPTON

In the weeks leading up to the Brexit referendum, Michael Gove, then justice secretary, appeared on Sky News to make the case for Britain leaving the European Union. Refusing to name economists who backed the UK exit, Mr Gove argued that 'People in this country have had enough of experts from organisations with acronyms saying they know what is best and getting it consistently wrong.' The sentiment highlighted a growing phenomenon of contempt and disdain for specialists, reflected most clearly in Donald Trump's 'anti-analytic' administration, where relatively uninformed friends and family were put in charge of entire government departments.

The word 'expert' comes from the Latin *expertus*, meaning 'having tested, proven or experienced'. Embedded in its etymology is the idea that proficiency is only possible through empirical research, rigorous study and time-honed discernment. Yet the rise of the internet has given people instant access to vast amounts of data, allowing them to develop hypotheses without needing any first-hand knowledge at all.

Much of this data is dubious. We inhabit a world in which careful analysis is afforded the same online exposure as dangerous propaganda and downright lies, and where powerful world leaders are believed when they dismiss uncomfortable truths as 'fake news'. With so much disinformation available at the click of a mouse, and billions of people engaged in a continuous global discussion, it is easier than ever to cherry-pick ideas that confirm personal bias, creating a wave of anti-rationalism. The current democratisation of knowledge should have made us all smarter, but instead it has helped foster a cult of ignorance in which people believe they know more than experts do.

A rise in affluence and education has also fuelled a general questioning in which people have stopped respecting professionals, believing that gut instinct trumps years of learning and training. Medics regularly complain they are competing with 'Doctor Google', with patients believing they know best, while there has been a rise of do-it-yourself websites and YouTube videos for everything from selling your home to fixing your boiler.

Ignorance has become an 'actual virtue', Tom Nichols writes in his book *The Death of Expertise: The Campaign Against Established Knowledge and Why it Matters*[1] and suggests that populism has given rise to a disdain for elites and experts from every walk of life. Curiously, when the book was published, back in 2017, Nichols predicted that it would take a global disaster – such as a horrendous war or a pandemic – to redress the balance. 'People will have to touch the hot stove of stupidity before they understand it's a bad idea,' he told the BBC[2].

Coronavirus has provided just such a global calamity and, at long last, has given some authority back to the experts. It is hard to be dismissive and contemptuous of someone who is trying to save your life, and rationalism has once again taken precedence over conspiracy theories and denialism.

From the beginning of the epidemic, politicians across the globe insisted that the response should be 'guided by science'. Never before have screens been so full of doctors and scientists outside television dramas. Never before has the public been so comfortable discussing death curves, attack rates and viral dynamics. At the daily briefings in Britain, ministers deferred to the chief medical officer, Chris Whitty, and the chief scientific advisor, Sir Patrick Vallance, who patiently took the public through graphs showing the progress of the virus.

And the lockdown compliance figures showed just how much the public was trusting the experts to keep them safe. In some towns in the UK, 98.4 per cent of people said they were following guidelines to stay home and protect the NHS. Research from 50,000 responses to the Evergreen Life health app showed that, even the least compliant area, Middlesbrough – where 25 per cent of people were ignoring restrictions – is still within the government's 75 per cent target[3].

As the weeks and months passed, anyone who was interested could access detailed modelling, projections, tolls of daily deaths and admissions, and testing statistics. Little was kept out of the public gaze, allowing people to draw their own conclusions based on not only the data but also their own experiences. The usual stifling and tedious peer-review process was abandoned in favour of fast, real-time science that allowed the public to understand the to-and-fro nature of research and deliberation before consensus is reached.

In a way, we have all become coronavirus experts, having lived through it and seen first-hand how the death rates plummeted as lockdown was enforced. We watched as the data emerged, and shifted, and altered. The pandemic has been a great lesson in nuance and in coming to a conclusion based on the evidence.

The pinnacle of the resistance to anti-expert rhetoric came in April, when there was widespread outcry after Donald Trump suggested that injecting yourself with disinfectant would kill off coronavirus. It was the moment when the US President's scientific illiteracy moved from risible to lethal. Injecting disinfectant at the levels needed to see off the virus would cause severe tissue burns, irreversible blood vessel damage and probable death. The press briefing led Reckitt Benckiser, the company that manufactures Dettol and Lysol, to issue a statement urging people not to drink or inject their products. The comments also caused a spike in calls to poison-control centres in Illinois, Maryland, Michigan and New York from people reporting exposure to household cleaners and disinfectants. And a man was hospitalised in Atlanta after drinking a pint of bleach to prevent coronavirus.

Trump undoubtedly suffers from the Dunning-Kruger effect, in which the most unqualified people for a given task believe they are the most capable. Or, as Socrates put it, 'Only the wise understand their own ignorance or fallibility.' Crucially, hundreds of experts came together to speak out and condemn Trump's comments in a global consensus of opinion that forced the president to row back on his words, claiming he was being sarcastic. It was a rare triumph of academia against administration.

So perhaps the post-truth era is not as troubling as it once was. In summer 2019, researchers at the University of Sheffield found that in fact there is broad public support for experts[4]. Coronavirus can only have improved this view. Even Mr Gove solemnly reassured the public that the government was now deferring to the best expert advice.

Those 'organisations with acronyms' are enjoying some long-overdue limelight, and the world will be better and safer for it.

Notes

1. OUP USA, 2017
2. https://www.bbc.co.uk/programmes/w3cswgwd
3. https://www.telegraph.co.uk/science/2020/04/05/coronavirus-can-sunbathing-spread-virus-should-ban-outdoor-exercise/

   Knapton, S., 'Coronavirus: Can Sunbathing Spread The Virus And Should We Ban Outdoor Exercise?' Telegraph, 5 April 2020
4. https://www.sheffield.ac.uk/news/nr/no-evidence-public-have-had-enough-of-experts-1.846832

   University of Sheffield, 'No Evidence That Public Have "Had Enough Of Experts", Study Finds' 3 June 2019

HEALTHCARE? IT'S AN APP

ALEX HERN

You carry in your pocket a slice of science fiction. One day, it will be a piece of etymological trivia as to why we call that slab of metal, glass and plastic a 'phone'. For now, it serves to disguise how wildly capable these devices actually are.

A screen, more vivid and higher resolution than the most expensive television you could buy thirty years ago. A camera, outclassing all but a dedicated SLR even today. A storage capacity of a few dozen libraries, or the largest record store you ever went to – if you cheap out and buy a basic model. And, of course, an always-on connection to the sum total of human creation and knowledge.

A typical phone also has at least four different types of wireless radio. One is set to receive-only, listens for the simple broadcasts of the constellation of GPS satellites constantly in orbit around the globe and uses a mixture of basic trigonometry and advanced physics to calculate the phone's exact location. Another connects to the mobile network. It's high-power, heavily regulated and spans a range of frequencies to broadcast to mobile phone masts that are potentially miles away. A third connects to Wi-Fi networks, a chaotic mid-range set of standards that somehow works (though often doesn't) to provide fast internet in our homes and offices. And a fourth, Bluetooth, uses minimal power to connect over short ranges with enough bandwidth to transmit audio, but not much more.

And so it might be surprising that, of all the wonderful features of a modern phone, it's the last of these that has the most potential to help fight coronavirus.

There's a lot that can be done directly with phones to help healthcare during a pandemic. Remote consultations can keep GP surgeries open without risking infection; donated devices allow isolation wards to be slightly less isolating for those stuck in them; widespread symptom-tracking allows for the spread of the infection to be monitored and new symptoms to be uncovered.

But at the beginning of the crisis, the most important thing wasn't really the healthcare itself: it was the data required to understand and combat the spread of the disease. And if there's one thing that phones are extremely good at, it's gathering data.

The first wave of questions was around movement. How were people adapting to the needs of social distancing? Were their patterns of behaviour changing, and if so, how? Did greater restrictions need to be implemented, or would these create invisible problems down the line?

The GPS receiver is perfect for answering those questions,

but brings with it its own problems. Gathering the exact location, to the metre, of each person in a whole country to work out if they're staying at home or going to the pub is at best using a sledgehammer to crack a walnut, and at worst, making a decision that can't be undone.

That's not to say that some didn't try. The Centers for Disease Control and Prevention in the US reportedly[1] gathered some GPS data from the mobile advertising industry, which had been collecting it for years thanks to questionable consent granted by users of weather apps, mobile games and the like.

But in the UK, we went for a simpler approach, using another quirk of phones: the fact that, to make them work, the mobile networks need to have a vague idea of where they are at any time.

Your phone is constantly yelling its name into the void. It's only trying to speak to the closest mast, but because it can't target its screams, it's heard by every nearby tower. That means that the phone needs to make clear which mast it's speaking to, and needs a way of working out when to switch to a new one. The converse is also true: the masts need to be able to keep track of which phones are their responsibility so they can hand over as their users move about. (If you've struggled to use your phone on a fast train, this is why: above a certain speed, these handovers simply happen too frequently for the network to keep up).

In the UK, the networks agreed to hand over this bulk data to the government, in order to let it see whether residential areas were steadily holding more people and whether city centres were emptying out.

In Israel, the government went one step further, switching on a system using the same techniques that had been built by Shin Bet, the country's counterintelligence agency, for tracking suspects. The idea was simple: if you could track members of the public, you could follow a new infection back and see who else the individual interacted with. It's a digital twist on the practice of contact tracing, which has long been part of the toolbox for dealing with the early and later stages of an outbreak of an infectious disease.

Unfortunately, the execution of the Israelis' plan left something to be desired, in part because revealing to your entire population that you had secretly built a mass-surveillance infrastructure and had turned it on without consultation is the worst way possible to achieve mass consent for the extraordinary measures required to tackle a pandemic. But also, it turns out that the accuracy such a system can provide simply isn't enough.

Covid-19 spreads, we think, through droplets in the air that can arc for a couple of metres from someone when they cough, sing or shout. But even the most accurate mobile network data is only tens of metres. That's the difference between being notified when you're sitting next to someone on the bus and being notified when you're waiting in the same train station.

GPS data would do better, but falls at the same hurdle of public trust: it is, probably rightly, hard to get everyone to agree to upload their location data to the government. That might feel unfair if you are the government, since most of those same people voluntarily upload their location data to Google every day.

But the upside is that it's not location data we need, it's interaction data. It's not important to know *where* two people met if you know when they met.

And so Bluetooth's weaknesses become its strength. The short range and low power means that it's possible for a phone to carry on constantly screaming its name, but only so that those who get very close are able to hear it. Each phone can remember it's been near the other, and then, if you later find you've been infected with coronavirus, it's possible to pull up a list of all the other phones you've been near and warn them all they may have been exposed.

This, more or less, is how digital contact tracing, also known as exposure notification, works. It comes in different flavours: the most popular, pushed by Apple and Google, adds in a lot of privacy-focused flourishes to ensure that it's impossible for a centralised authority to use the system for any sort of tracking. Other versions, like those used in Singapore and Australia, are slightly simpler, and share a bit more information with the state in return.

However they work, it's hard to see a future where such systems don't play a key role in limiting resurgence of the virus. There are difficulties to overcome: not everyone has a phone, not everyone with a phone will install the required apps, and not everyone who does install the apps will remember to carry their charged phone with them everywhere.

But just as the exponential growth in infections led to the terrifying steepness of the curve at the beginning of the crisis, so it also boosts the efficacy of any intervention, no matter how minor. One person getting a notification that they have been exposed to Covid-19 and staying inside for the most infectious period might save only two others who would otherwise have caught the disease, but those two people in turn won't infect a further four, who won't infect a further eight, and so on down the chain. It's only the beginning, but it's a way out.

Notes

1. https://www.wsj.com/articles/government-tracking-how-people-move-around-in-coronavirus-pandemic-11585393202

    Tau, B., 'Government Tracking How People Move Around in Coronavirus Pandemic' *Wall Street Journal*, 28 March 2020

PARENTS

LUCY MANGAN

'Listen to me: you're not going. And that's my final word.'

'Fine,' the voice muttered mutinously on the other end of the line. 'If you're going to be like this, I won't.'

'Damn right you won't!' And we each put the phone down. I felt battered and bruised but strangely exhilarated. For I had just been part of a complete role reversal. We were heading into lockdown and my mother had just given me her plans for the day, which involved going to Sainsbury's for some food, a trip to Bromley for some trousers and a coffee 'just with Marian, just at Dunelm'. And it was I who had been laying down the law and my parents who had capitulated.

It was a pattern being repeated up and down the land. Grown-up children were suddenly having not only to explain the new rules to their offspring, but also to impress their importance upon the generation above. For some reason only we, the sandwiched middle, seemed to feel mortal in the face of a brand-new zoonotic virus of definite, recorded lethality.

Other things changed, too. Suddenly it was up to us to put food on our parents' table. At a distance, sure, and via online monitoring of scarce delivery slots briefly available from various supermarkets or by following up Facebook tips and social media whispers about increasingly outré outlets who had just pivoted to delivery to try and meet the need, rather than the nine-to-five job they had done to earn the money to bang down plates of fish fingers and chips five nights a week. But it was unsettling, nevertheless.

But to become unsettled is not the worst thing that can happen. Sometimes being unsettled is an opportunity for change – needed, necessary, healthy change – especially, perhaps, in family dynamics, which tend to be decided in the early years and become carved deeper in stone with every further year that passes. Among the classic set-ups, of course, are to have the 'fun' parent and the strict one, the 'clever' child and the one that's not, the sporty and the bookish, the dutiful one and the flibbertigibbet. And so each is looked to at certain times for certain things, and your path and role (at least within the family, though these things have a remarkable way of also playing themselves out beyond that) is set. Rare is the chance for a reset that does not involve bereavement, dementia or some kind of cataclysmic, deep rupture from within the family unit. Pandemic conditions, however, offer a third way. You can realign yourselves and your relationships in order to battle an external enemy, rather than identify – or appear to identify – ones within. It's the difference between having a bomb land on your house during the Blitz and blowing it up yourself. You'd get a new house either way but people would only let you live in it blamelessly via the former method.

For my own part, the pandemic has forced me out of my complacency and my comfort zone where my parents are concerned. They are not getting any younger. They are not the oracles they always seemed in my youth and that part of me has always cleaved to believing they remain. They do not always know best – not for me; not for themselves. Probably this is a revelation I should have had decades ago, maybe during a rebellious teenager-hood or at university, when I was supposedly being intellectually expanded. But I've never been much of a one for rebellion or intellectual expansion – and anyway, parents and parental bonds seem to exist outside the rational world.

My sister – long known, and rightly so, as the endlessly practical, preternaturally competent one – of course, did her usual sterling work in working out logistics, upgrading technology and talking resistant near-octogenarians through installing apps that meant we could communicate and keep better tabs on them, in between sewing facemasks for us and most of her village, as the new rules for living began to constrain us all. But, d'you know what? It turned out that I had my uses, too. As well as tracking down food, I found help from the council for all those who were shielding, worked out their GP's new system for consultations now that no face-to-face contact could happen, and so on and so forth. And I overturned forty years of dedicated training so I could manage the previously inconceivable feat of arguing with my progenitors. I alerted them when they were still thinking too large ('Dunelm? Are you mad? You might as well go to a Marrakech souk! Kitchen – the kitchen is where you go for coffee. From now until I tell you otherwise!') and digested and regurgitated a wider array of news, information and likely forthcoming measures than could be delivered by the *Guardian* in the morning and five minutes of the ten o'clock news before bed.

And once the initial shock of this tectonic shift has worn off, a strange kind of excitement mounts as you look out onto the altered landscape. What else, you wonder, did you assume was as unalterable as the mountains but turns out to be mutable after all? What else, what other relationships, or parts thereof, have you accepted as natural but are in fact a product of circumstance, habit and subconscious nurture, like everything else? What else, in short, might be up for grabs?

There is, to be sure, not much to be said for life under lockdown. But it does afford us a rare pause, a rare chance to take stock of our lives and of the structures they are built on rather than just the superficial concerns of the day-to-day. A moment to question what really might be within our power to change, individually and, on from that – when we're out the other side of this – collectively; to decide what remains fit for purpose and what could, even if we have never considered it before, be jettisoned, for our own or for the greater good.

I have assured my mother, however, that whatever happens, coffee and Dunelm will endure.

ARTIFICIAL MEAT

TOM WHIPPLE

At about the same time that the Chinese government was closing restaurants in Wuhan, in Israel a group of diners were tasting a really average steak.

This steak had, the first volunteers said, a 'typical meat bite and texture,' but even a late night doner kebab shop would have termed the next comment only 'faint praise'. It was notable, they decided, for having the 'pleasant ... sensorial attributes' of meat.

These two events, the lockdown and the mediocre meal, do not initially appear to be linked. But in their coincidence – an alignment of both technology and the need for that technology – could yet herald one of the great revolutions of the twenty-first century.

Because while that steak might have been very mediocre, what set it apart – made it, in fact, a culinary triumph – was that it was made in a laboratory. It was also, unlike the kinds of meat substitute you may be familiar with, not a substitute. It was, unambiguously, made from cow. As the volunteers tore strips of meat and chewed on fried flesh, every bit of muscle they ate was cow muscle – but it was cow muscle that had never roamed through a field or been nourished by grass. It was a bit small, and a bit funny-tasting, but it was the closest thing anyone has seen to a true laboratory steak.

Artificial meat has been one of those ideas that has been the next big thing for a very long time. Winston Churchill made the case for lab-grown meat as early as 1930. For an essay in *The Strand Magazine* he predicted that by 1980, 'We shall escape the absurdity of growing a whole chicken in order to eat the breast or wing, by growing these parts separately under a suitable medium.'

He was referring to the sheer wastefulness of having a walking, squawking bird expending energy on gizzards, heart, brain, lungs and the aforementioned walking and squawking when as a consumer you want none of that. But there is another more compelling reason to separate a breast or a rump from the animal that makes it. That is because in that animal – in its lungs and heart and sometimes even its brain – is a medium in which disease can spread. In the industrial farms where the animals are packed together at a constant temperature are the perfect conditions to incubate a disease outbreak. Then, with just the smallest mutation, that outbreak can spread to humans and conquer the world.

Forty years after Churchill's deadline passed, his goal has only just been achieved – and making it commercially viable is still proving extremely challenging. Using stem cells, it is possible to culture real muscle cells, but difficult to do so at scale. It is also hard to mix them with the kind of juicier cell that gives meat its taste: fat cells. Without a blood supply, each strip of meat is extremely thin, and with only a single cell type the resulting burgers – if you only have thin strips, a burger is the best you can do – haven't always tasted very impressive.

In a laboratory in the Israel Institute of Technology, however, Professor Shulamit Levenberg realised there was another way. She and her colleagues had been developing human muscle, grown from patients' own cells then grafted back into the abdomen. To do this, you can't just plonk in a human burger patty. To be useful the graft needs structure, complexity, a three-dimensional shape. The scientists had created this using a scaffold of soy protein.

The work was, needless to say, of great importance for the health system. It was only later that the team made the mental leap to realise they could also apply their technique to fast food. It's not surprising it took them a while. You don't, in general, spend tens of thousands of pounds manufacturing an exquisitely complex, high-technology medical intervention only to then stick it on a griddle.

Soon, though, the scientists hope their research will be on everyone's griddle. Collaborating with a commercial partner, Professor Levenberg thinks they can get real steaks, but ones that have never seen a cow's rump, onto the world's tables.

They are not the only ones doing this. Nor are they the only ones commercialising it. In the US, Memphis Meats has raised $200m to produce artificial beef, from backers including Richard Branson and Bill Gates. Just along the coast from Memphis Meats' California headquarters, Finless Foods is trying to do the same with fish. Their view is that the first artificial meat will be expensive, so why not make something that people already pay a lot for – sushi. After all, it's as easy to cultivate the steak of an endangered tuna as it is a broiler chicken.

In their quest to persuade the world that they are the future, the meat manufacturers have made two arguments, neither of which has, so far, seemed to persuade consumers. The first is environmental. A cow, they say, is a very inefficient way of making food. For every kilogram of protein you put into a cow, just thirty grams makes it into a human. For each kilogram of beef the cow makes, 15,000 litres of water are needed. Meanwhile, each cow on the planet requires two acres of land. If your sole goal was to make calories, you would not choose to pass those calories – in the form of animal feed – through a cow first.

The second is ethics. Much of farming is not pleasant for the animal. It is so unpleasant, in fact, that most of us choose not to find out how unpleasant – preferring ignorance to the moral muddiness that would come with full knowledge of the process of the animals' birth, hormone-assisted rearing and slaughter.

With coronavirus, however, there comes a third, possibly even more persuasive, argument: self-interest. Pandemics are caused by an unholy trinity: humans in large dense cities, easy travel between those cities and animals in close proximity to humans. Most of the diseases humans have experienced in the past 10,000 years started in animals, gained a foothold in settlements, and then spread via trade routes.

We are not going to stop living in cities, nor are we going to stop travelling. With artificial meat, though, we can put an end to livestock farming – and arguably complete a process begun 20,000 years ago.

Farming is strange. The agricultural revolution was the first great human civilisational advance. Domestication – of crops and animals – was the base on which everything else was built. The odd thing is, though, that's where it stayed. Yes there have been advances, but if you took the world's first farmer from the banks of the Euphrates and put them on a modern farm among a herd of modern cows, and they would understand pretty quickly what was going on. Planes and computers have, by contrast, existed for less than 1 per cent of the time we have been farming. But show the same farmer a silicon chip or an aeroplane and it would be indistinguishable from magic.

Now, in the petri dishes of the world's stem cell biologists, in the 'pleasant sensorial attributes' of the meat they make, we have the opportunity to bring some of that scientific magic to farming. After coronavirus, we might just have the impetus too.

THE ACT OF GIVING

LINDSAY DODGSON

The act of giving to those in need has taken on a new meaning in recent months. Whether it's vast sums of money donated by the world's richest, or everyday people dedicating their spare time to those who are struggling the most, the coronavirus pandemic has set a new tone for how generosity can really be valued.

While the collective stress caused by the sudden chaos has certainly contributed to growing anxieties and panic across the world, it has also led to a greater sense of togetherness. Thousands of people have volunteered to help the NHS by signing up as phone responders, to help set up food redistribution centres and to deliver necessities to the elderly and vulnerable.

Life coach and motivational speaker Michael Cloonan said he has been offering his services for free to key workers to help them cope with the toll their jobs are taking on their mental health. He said he has been picking up the phone to anyone in need, even if it's just so they take away a snippet of advice – a breathing technique, or learning to hold their body in a way that can make them feel more positive.[1] 'Anything I can do to help people . . .' he said. 'I have a passion for people – that's my thing. People just want to talk. So you give them small things to do to change their approach, to change their mindset and stuff, and it can be really good.'

There's also been a huge global philanthropy effort among the world's richest people. Twitter co-founder Jack Dorsey, for example, donated $1 billion of his fortune from his payment firm Square, while countless celebrities, such as Blake Lively, Ryan Reynolds and Leonardo DiCaprio, have donated millions of dollars and even set up foundations to help food banks, supply equipment to essential workers and fund efforts to develop a coronavirus vaccine.[2]

In the online world, YouTubers have been giving back to their loyal audiences who may be struggling. Stars such as Tana Mongeau and Jeffree Star have been sending money to their fans through cash transfer apps, while David Dobrik drove around firing $10,000 cheques out of a cannon at people who had asked for his help.

One online star, Jimmy Donaldson, better known as MrBeast, hosted the most famous game of rock paper scissors in history as a fundraiser, involving some of YouTube's most famous faces, such as Casey Neistat, KSI and Ninja. Even Jack Black made an appearance. The live stream amassed over $1,000,000 in donations towards the World Health Organization through small acts of charity from people watching the event.

When added together, the sheer scale of all these philanthropic and volunteering efforts over the last few months shows the immense ability we have to support one another. It's hard not to be optimistic about what that could mean both for the global population and for each of us as individuals.

Reaching out to show care for others has numerous benefits to both our psychology and physiology, according to Dr Louise Joy-Johnson, a clinical psychologist at the Priory Wellbeing Centre in Manchester. She says connecting with others and tending to their needs activates our 'social safety and soothing' system, which triggers the release of happy hormones such as oxytocin. It's a tactic often used in therapy to treat mental health problems, because it helps people learn to direct kindness and compassion towards themselves and others as an alternative to internalising judgement and anger.

'Learning to be kind to ourselves and others can be difficult, especially when we have experienced traumatic events in life,' Joy-Johnson says. 'But by engaging in activities such as volunteering, we get to step out of our own heads and struggles, and be present, in a very healing way, with others.' Joy-Johnson says the responses to our actions, and spending time with others, helps us feel to valued as a human being because these are 'fundamental emotional needs, essential for maintaining and optimising our mental health and wellbeing.'

Being kind can also help the 'fight, flight, freeze' response in our brain, which is heightened during any crisis. We are all hyper-aware and overstimulated right now because there are so many things we need to worry about on top of our regular stressors. This puts the bar for feeling anxious significantly lower than usual, with concerns about loved ones, employment and the world as a whole constantly bubbling under the surface.

Joy-Johnson says it's more important than ever that we share these burdens because feeling connected and comforted really can help lower our levels of cortisol – the stress hormone. 'These acts of kindness can help us to value a shared humanity, noticing we are more alike than we are different and are designed to share life's experiences, both good and bad,' she says. 'We are interconnected – when one suffers, we all suffer – and to heal and to flourish we need one another.'

The ripple effect of so many people being selfless and charitable could produce a more resilient and supportive society as we go forward, full of people who are more focused on the collective well-being.

Of course there's no guarantee for what the future will look like. In all likelihood, our idea of what is normal may be different for a long time. It may have even shifted for ever. But one positive of that comes from looking back and knowing we made the most of a bad, tragic or even hopeless-feeling situation by reaching out in any way possible to those less fortunate than ourselves. With that gratitude and improved awareness, we might even have learned to deal a little more effectively with the next challenge we face. Joy-Johnson says this is because humans are particularly skilled in looking for the good in hardship.

You don't need to be a billionaire or have a massive platform to make a difference in the world. The biggest stars and entrepreneurs may be doing their part with the more substantial tools and resources they have, but so is everyone else. Captain Sir Tom Moore, a former British Army officer, raised money for the NHS on the run-up to his 100th birthday. He began his twenty-four-day challenge of walking 100 25-metre laps of his garden in early April, with the goal of raising £1000. This modest target and brilliant effort struck a chord with the public and Moore quickly became a household name. He appeared on television and radio shows, and even featured in a fundraising cover version of the song 'You'll Never Walk Alone'.

When the campaign ended, on the morning of Moore's birthday, it had amassed over £32 million in total donations, earning him Royal Air Force flypasts, appointment as an honorary colonel of the Army Foundation College and a knighthood.

Moore told the BBC that the NHS workers deserved every penny because of their bravery; because we are facing something of a war right now, with key workers putting themselves in harm's way for the rest of us. 'The doctors and the nurses, they're all on the front line,' he said. 'And all of us behind, we've got to supply them and keep them going with everything that they need, so that they can do their jobs even better than they're doing now.'[3]

No kind deed should be dismissed, no matter how small you may think it is. Taking round some essential supplies to a neighbour, sending a letter to an older relative, or even just picking up the phone, could mean the world to someone, and that's a movement we should strive to continue. 'There has been great heartbreak, and losses, and many struggles will be ongoing,' says Dr Joy-Johnson. 'However, perhaps as we allow ourselves to grieve the losses and direct compassion and kindness towards ourselves and others during this time and beyond, we will bring much healing and well-being to the societies in which we live.'

Notes

1. https://www.mylondon.news/news/zone-1-news/
    london-coronavirus-live-amazing-things-18006927
    McKinnell, E. and Kane, H., 'London Coronavirus Live:
    The Amazing Things Londoners Are Doing Throughout the
    Coronavirus Crisis', *MyLondon*, 14 April 2020
2. https://www.insider.com/
    celebrities-coronavirus-donations-pandemic-relief-efforts-2020-3
    Singh, O., 'Celebrities Who Have Donated Money Amid the
    Coronavirus Pandemic', *Insider*, 26 May 2020
3. https://www.bbc.co.uk/news/av/uk-52296313/coronavirus-army-
    veteran-tom-moore-finds-out-he-s-raised-5m-for-nhs
    'Coronavirus: Army Veteran Tom Moore Finds Out He's
    Raised £5 Million for NHS', BBC News, 15 April 2020

RESILIENCE

SARAH KNAPTON

In 2019 scientists studying the physical and mental health of Holocaust survivors made a startling discovery. Despite the horrors of torture, the prolonged malnutrition and the daily grind of unhygienic, cold and damp concentration camps, those who made it through lived longer than others from the same era who were spared such atrocities.

While 41 per cent of a control group died during the study period of 1998–2017, 75 per cent of the Holocaust survivors were still alive. The researchers, from Maccabi Healthcare Services in Israel, concluded that the survivors may have built up a 'unique resilience' which boosted their desire to live and a resolve to look after themselves in later life. Oddly enough, it wasn't because they were naturally more healthy. Survivors tended to have more chronic illness, had suffered more heart attacks and had even reported more broken bones. But their conditions proved far less deadly, possibly because they took more interest in their health, identifying problems early and getting treatment before conditions spiralled past a point of no return. It is possible that coronavirus could also help build up levels of global resilience that will help people live healthier, happier and more productive lives when the crisis is finally over.

Although it is unfair to indiscriminately pin the 'snowflake' badge on millennials, in recent decades there has certainly been a cultural shift away from the hierarchical 'strict father' model of parenting and schooling to a more egalitarian 'nurturant' philosophy that has often left young people unprepared for the harsh realities of life. Such well-meaning care has created the need for trigger warnings on classic literature, for safe spaces and the no-platforming of even moderate speakers at universities.

But it's impossible to no-platform a deadly global disease, however upsetting and uncomfortable it might be. And that stark realisation could be hugely beneficial. Some things simply must be faced and lived through to build courage and a sense of fearlessness. The German philosopher Friedrich Nietzsche surmised, 'That which does not kill us makes us stronger', and Sigmund Freud also understood that suffering is an inevitable and crucial part of life.

The idea of emotional resilience – the word comes from the Latin *resilio*, which means to jump or bounce back – was popularised in the seventies by the American psychologist Emmy Werner while studying children from Kauai, an impoverished region of Hawaii. Two thirds were found to exhibit destructive behaviours in adulthood, whereas one third behaved normally, and Werner concluded that these children had genetic traits that protected them from the impact of poverty[1]. The idea that resilience was inbuilt rather than fostered remained prevalent for more than forty years, but by the beginning of this decade the pendulum was swinging back to Nietzschean thinking.

Now, after decades of health-and-safety edicts, some educators have started deliberately introducing risk into playgrounds to encourage self-sufficiency and practical thinking. The idea is not new. During the Second World War, the Danish landscape architect Carl Theodor Sørensen opened a series of 'junk playgrounds' after noticing children preferred to play in bomb sites. Likewise, in Britain, the rubble of certain collapsed buildings was opened up to children and remarketed as 'adventure playgrounds' to foster independence and risk analysis.

Psychologists have now discovered that while personal assaults, bereavements or natural disasters can be harmful to mental and physical health, smaller amounts of trauma actually help people develop resilience. Researchers at the State University of New York at Buffalo found that people who experienced a great deal of adversity were generally more distressed than others but those who had experienced no traumatic events had similar psychological problems. The people with the best outcomes were those who had experienced some negative events[2].

Psychologists believe traumatic experiences give people the opportunity to develop coping mechanisms and build friendship networks, which stand them in good stead for future troubles. Certainly in nature and evolution, it is life that can adapt to hardship and difficult times that succeeds in the long term. Making the body resilient to temporary starvation through fasting appears to reboot the entire immune system and may even slow down ageing. Muscles that are not worked get weaker; using it or losing it is a crucial part of how our bodies function. Bacteria that are not totally wiped out by antibiotics become resistant. Indeed, the success of coronavirus itself can be attributed to its ability to mutate when the going got tough.

Some will argue that those who have survived traumatic events, such as the Holocaust, may simply have been the strongest to begin with, both physically and mentally, a pattern that would inevitably play out in later life[3]. However, many psychologists believe that it is love, care and feeling part of a community that is the best method for toughening people up and building resilience. This support has been abundant during the coronavirus crisis: children's drawings of rainbows beamed out from windows across the UK; millions took to the streets each Thursday to clap for carers; companies put people before profits to design ventilators, face masks and tests to help the public sector; a country divided by Brexit suddenly felt united again in a common cause.

Emotional resilience is now widely taught by psychologists, and the Department of Health even has an online toolkit. But living through coronavirus has taught people such abstract lessons first-hand. It has encouraged people to see crises as challenges that can be overcome, rather than insurmountable problems. The hunt for a vaccine has demonstrated what countries and experts can achieve when they work together. The pandemic has demonstrated the importance of having a supportive network of friends and family, and will help people to accept that change isn't a disaster; it is part of life. It has given people the time and opportunity for self-improvement as well as for practising optimism in a bad situation, eating more healthily and sleeping longer, and for enforced relaxation.

If you're reading this, you are getting through it – or have got through it. So don't be surprised if life feels a little bit easier now. This new emotional resilience has been hard won, but maybe it's time to acknowledge that coronavirus has made you a little tougher, a little wiser and perhaps even a little happier.

Notes

1. https://www.newyorker.com/science/maria-konnikova/
    the-secret-formula-for-resilience
    Konnikova, M. 'How People Learn to Become Resilient' *New Yorker*, 11 February 2016
2. Seery, M. D., Holman, E. A. and Silver, R. C., 'Whatever Does Not Kill Us: Cumulative Lifetime Adversity, Vulnerability, and Resilience', *Journal of Personality and Social Psychology*, December 2010, Vol.99(6), pp.1025–41.
3. Seery, M. D., Holman, E. A. and Silver, R. C., 'Whatever Does Not Kill Us: Cumulative Lifetime Adversity, Vulnerability, and Resilience', *Journal of Personality and Social Psychology*, December 2010, Vol.99(6), pp.1025–41

WE GOT LUCKY

TOM WHIPPLE

The coronavirus outbreak has been a pandemic of superlatives: the greatest peacetime economic crisis since, by some counts, the 1700s; the biggest public health crisis since 1918; the fastest-spreading disease since . . . ever. But it could have been so much worse.

It seems strange to say that we have been lucky; stranger still to say that, in the end, this virus – this microscopic string of protein that stopped the world – might just save lives. But it might. To understand why, you need to consider another virus, a virus you may have missed.

For aeons, this other virus spread between birds. It soared over mountains, glided over forests and fled the snows of winter as it hitched a ride with birds' migrations. Later, it found a less romantic – but far more climate-controlled and productive – home amid poultry, in farms where chickens were packed wing to wing.

Then, in the early part of this century, this particular virus learned to spread into another species: humans. This virus was not coronavirus. It was avian influenza, H5N1. In February 2020 Steven Chu, cellular scientist, Nobel Laureate and former secretary of energy to President Obama, was asked about his concerns around the growing coronavirus pandemic. He talked, instead, about avian flu. 'This is something even more worrisome, if you'd like to worry,' he said, noting a new cluster of infections just that week, in a province just north of Wuhan. 'If you get it you have a 60 per cent chance of dying.' So far, whenever there has been an outbreak it has not mutated to spread between humans. If it did, said Professor Chu, it would be 'big-time serious stuff.'[1]

Coronavirus could indeed have been a lot worse.

No one can pretend we hadn't been warned that this could happen. In 2015, Bill Gates gave a talk about pandemic risk. 'If anything kills over 10 million people in the next few decades, it's most likely to be a highly infectious virus rather than a war,' he said.

This was not a controversial statement – among virologists and microbiologists it had become orthodoxy – and nor is it new. Half a century ago, the Nobel Prize-winning biologist Joshua Lederberg put it more bluntly: 'The single biggest threat to man's continued dominance on this planet is the virus,' he said. Gates and Lederberg were of course ignored.

It took the real thing – coronavirus – for the world to finally come together in defeating an infectious disease; to pool its resources to fight the viral enemy. The scientific fightback has been yet another superlative, but this time a positive one: the greatest international research collaboration in history. Two weeks after China notified the world it had a new disease, that virus's genetic code was sequenced. A month after that, the first potential vaccines were being tested on animals. Using innovative techniques, researchers constructed new drugs using just the genetics of the virus. So it was that a process that normally takes years had been compressed into weeks. The world had, for the first time, developed a vaccine production line – one that could, in theory, be applied to any future virus.

Elsewhere, in the USA, Taiwan, Europe and New Zealand, teams of researchers were teasing out the other secrets of coronavirus. Before the northern hemisphere's winter was over, hundreds of research papers had been written – and, crucially, quickly published online – detailing the virus's history, how it had infected people and even what it looked like. In the past, academics were secretive about their data, hoarding it until they could publish in the most prestigious journals. Now that whole way of working has been blown apart.

In a race against a disease, a virus will always outrun humans in the first stretch – but we have found ways to get out of the blocks faster. We have managed this because, while you can ignore warnings, you can't ignore a pandemic. It took this deadly virus for us to listen to the words of the scientists who had prophesied just such an event.

In the midst of a global disaster, it is hard to appreciate the fact that we were lucky. It will, most likely, not cause the tens, even hundreds, of millions of deaths some said was possible.

But it could have. Coronavirus has, according to our best estimates, a fatality rate of 1–2 per cent and an infectiousness of around 3 – meaning that each person infected at the start of an outbreak passes it on to three others. Those who do die are disproportionately – but not exclusively – the old and sick.

Smallpox had a fatality rate of 30 per cent and an infectiousness of about 5. The Spanish Flu had a comparable infectiousness to coronavirus and a slightly higher fatality rate. It also had the peculiarity that those most affected included people in their twenties and thirties. You don't have to be one of those ultra-rationalist utilitarians who put a precise value on years of life to think that there is a particular tragedy in an illness where the old bury the young.

The point is not to be grateful that coronavirus isn't worse. Instead it is to realise those worse options – the viruses that kill more and spread faster – are still there. Before they come, the world has been trained – and warned. What we do next is our choice. It may be that, in the hard years to come, we forget what we have learned, we weaken international institutions and bicker about blame. If we do all these then viruses, which are no respecters of borders, will come back again.

But there is another path. This virus has shown us just what we can do. It has shown us that, whatever the animus of their national governments, a team of researchers in Beijing can collaborate with one in Seattle. In a matter of days, a team in Oxford can use Chinese data to make a potential vaccine from first principles. Then another team in Australia can use the same data to tease out the process by which the virus attacks the respiratory system. Viruses don't respect borders; neither does science.

Coronavirus has been an utterly terrible disease. It has also been just about the most benign disease you could conceive that would make the world finally sit up and take notice of the power of pandemics. Next time, we will be ready.

Notes

1.   AAAS Conference, 2020

Contributors

Graham Davey is Emeritus Professor of Psychology at the University of Sussex. His main research interests include the causes of anxiety, anxiety-based problems, and pathological worrying. He is currently Editor-in-Chief of *The Journal of Experimental Psychopathology*. He has written or edited a number of books on these and related topics including *The Anxiety Epidemic* (2018), *Psychology* (2018), *Psychopathology* (2014), and *Applied Psychology* (2008), and has a regular *Psychology Today* blog. He is a former President of the British Psychological Society, an avid consumer of real ales and curries, and a long-suffering supporter of Leicester City Football Club.

Lindsay Dodgson is a senior reporter at *Insider* in London. She's a sociable introvert who loves house plants, yoga, and long talks with old friends, followed by ten hours of sleep. She studied Zoology at university, then completed a masters degree in Science Journalism. She's written about lots of different things, including space, drugs, and sex, but more recently has settled on reporting about the internet and digital culture.

She likes to think she sensitively tells people's personal stories while bringing awareness to mental health conditions and the human psyche. Her aim is to help people understand why they behave in certain ways, both on and offline.

Alex Hern is the *Guardian*'s UK technology editor. He's chronicled the rise of TikTok, the death of Nokia, and the creation of the new tech oligopoly, as well as making his own cryptocurrency, living a day in virtual reality, and reading all the small print on the internet. He also wrote that Bitcoin was in a bubble when it cost $38, which was only wrong by $15,000. He lives in East London with his partner Cheryl and a small but rapidly growing collection of potted plants and painted miniatures.

Sarah Knapton is Science Editor at the *Daily Telegraph*. After completing a degree in Archaeology at the University of Newcastle, she moved to the *Newcastle Evening Chronicle* as a general news reporter, then worked as a court reporter at the Central Criminal Court (The Old Bailey) before moving to the *Guardian* as a senior reporter. In 2008 she moved to the *Telegraph*, working as a senior reporter, assistant news editor and executive editor of *Telegraph Online*, before becoming Science Correspondent in 2013 and Science Editor in 2015. In 2019, she was named Society of Editors Science Journalist of the Year and was Highly Commended in 2020. She is a qualified yoga teacher and a keen sailor.

Lucy Mangan is an award-winning columnist, the *Guardian* TV critic and author. Her most recent publication is *Bookworm: a Memoir of Childhood Reading*. She lives in London with several thousand books and a husband, son and two cats who conspire to keep her from any of them.

Tom Whipple is the science editor at *The Times*. His career has taken him to the top of Mont Blanc and to the tunnels beneath Cern. He has investigated the effects of radiation in the forests around Chernobyl, and the effects of heat in the world's hottest sauna in Finland. He didn't stay in very long. In the course of doing his job he has been arrested by the Danish police and the Tamil Tigers. The latter were a lot more polite. He has a mathematics degree.